Maps of Fictional Places

40 Inspiring Templates to Sketch and Plan your Locations

created by
Abria Mattina

Contents

Contents

Contents

WELCOME TO YOUR BOOK OF MAPS OF FICTIONAL PLACES

Whether you're a writer, an artist, a gamer, or a role-player, I hope you find this book of map templates inspiring and useful.

The Maps of Fictional Places book contains forty map templates and legends in four styles: landscapes, planets, cities and man-made structures, and islands. The legends include lists to record cities and towns, landmarks (e.g. mountains, rivers, etc.), bodies of water, and provinces and districts. Keep track of your own markings, such as roadways, with the Lines & Symbols space. You'll also find blank pages for notes, rough drafts, or anything else about your creations you wish to record.

Landscape and Island pages are designed with plain lines, which make it easy to interpret the landforms and bodies of water any way you wish. The scale of these maps is entirely up to you – map a single city or an entire continent. Coastlines and other natural borders are rendered in varying amounts of detail, for those who want minute topography and those who just want the broad strokes.

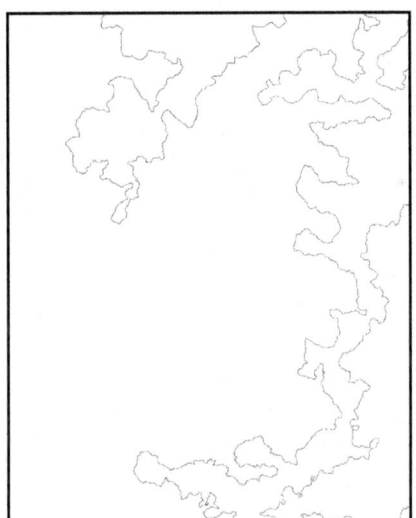 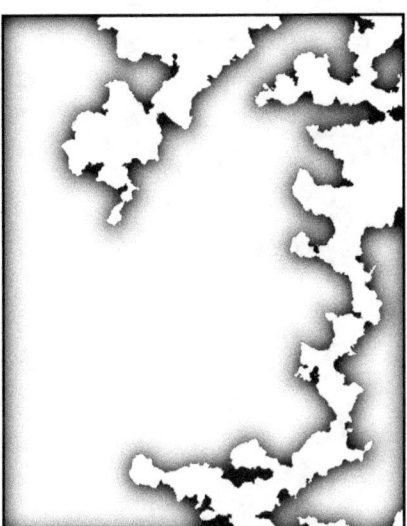 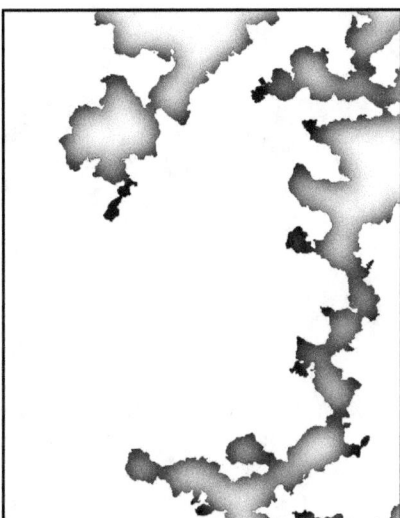

Share your creations on Twitter or Instagram, @AbriaMattina.

Landscapes

The voyage of discovery is not in seeking new landscapes but
in having new eyes.

Marcel Proust

MAP

Story:

Cities

Landmarks

_____

_____

_____

_____

_____

Bodies of Water

Provinces/Districts

_____

_____

_____

_____

Lines and Symbols

Scale

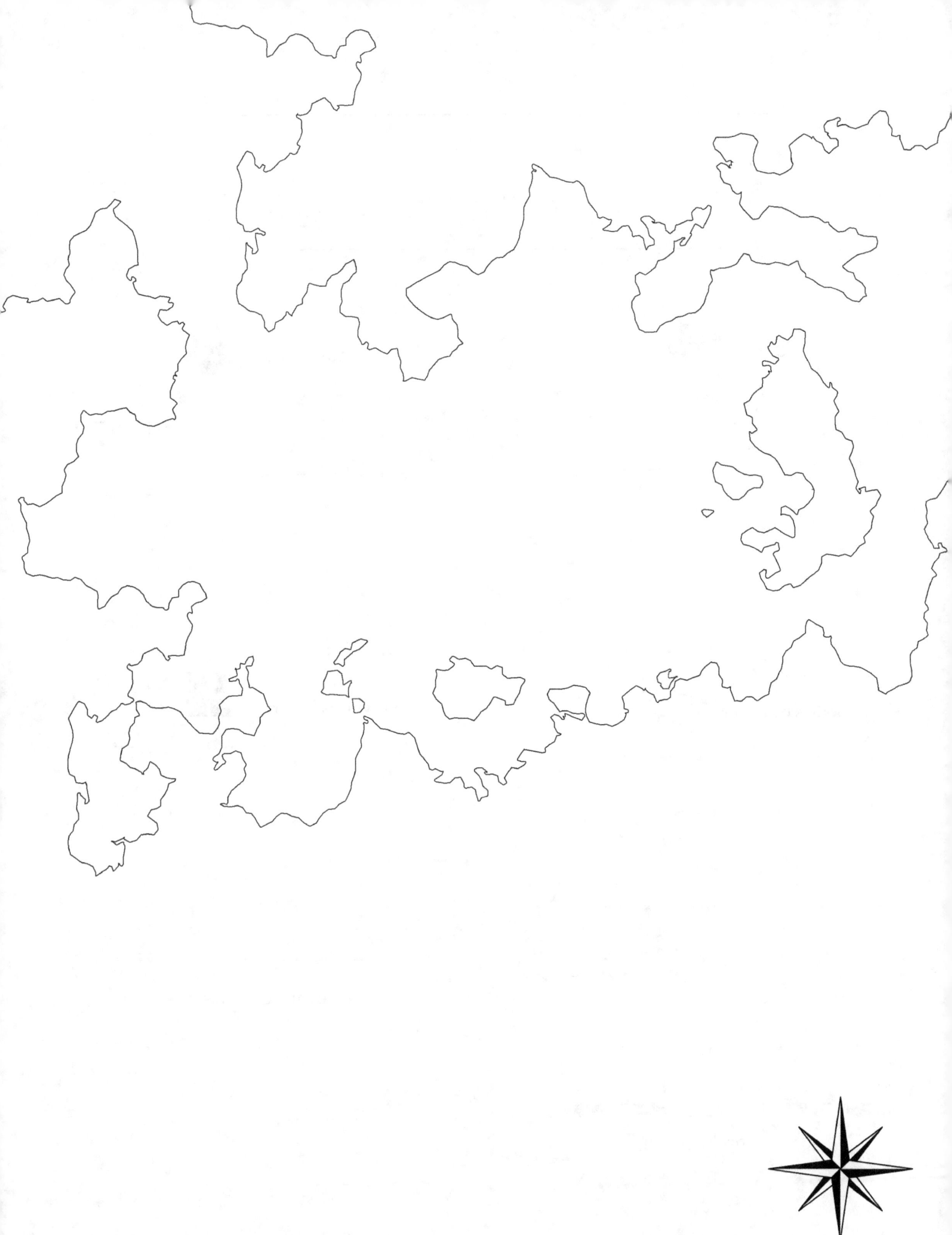

M A P

Story:

_____

Cities

_____
_____
_____
_____

Landmarks

_____
_____
_____
_____

Bodies of Water

_____
_____
_____
_____

Provinces/Districts

_____
_____
_____
_____

Lines and Symbols

Scale

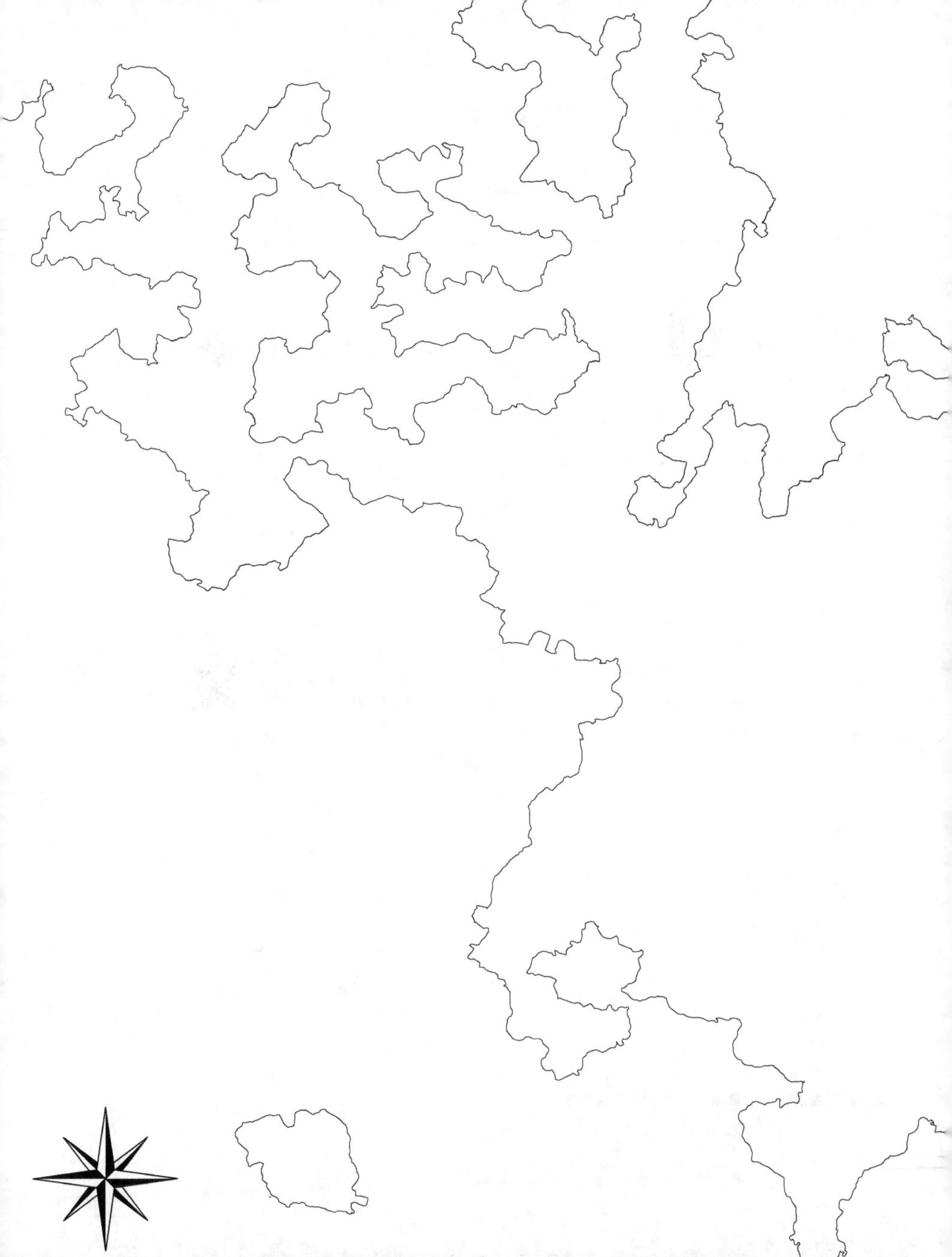

MAP

Story:

_____

Cities

_____
_____
_____
_____
_____

Landmarks

_____
_____
_____
_____
_____

Bodies of Water

_____
_____
_____
_____
_____

Provinces/Districts

_____
_____
_____
_____
_____

Lines and Symbols

Scale

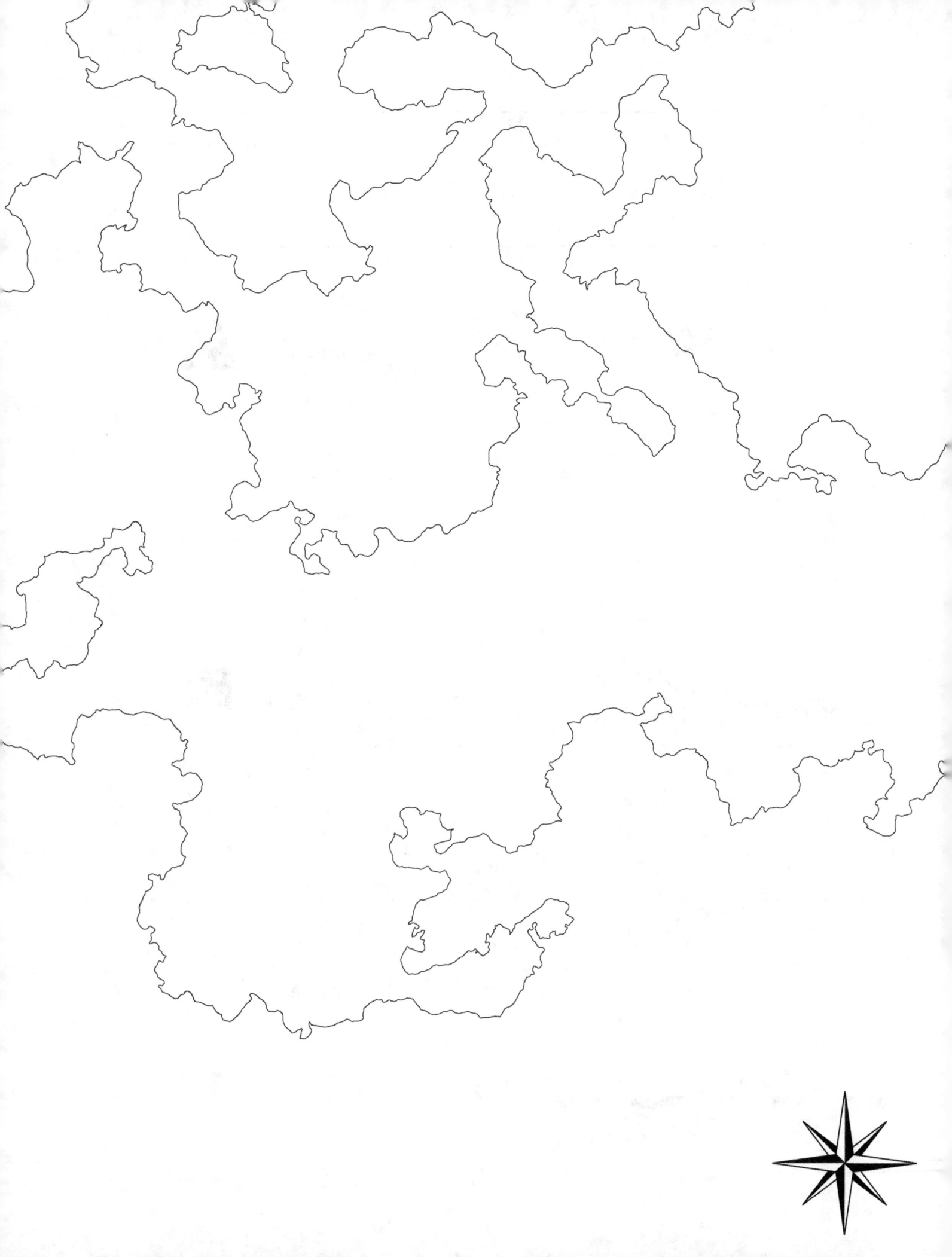

M A P

Story:

_____

Cities

Landmarks

Bodies of Water

Provinces/Districts

Lines and Symbols

Scale

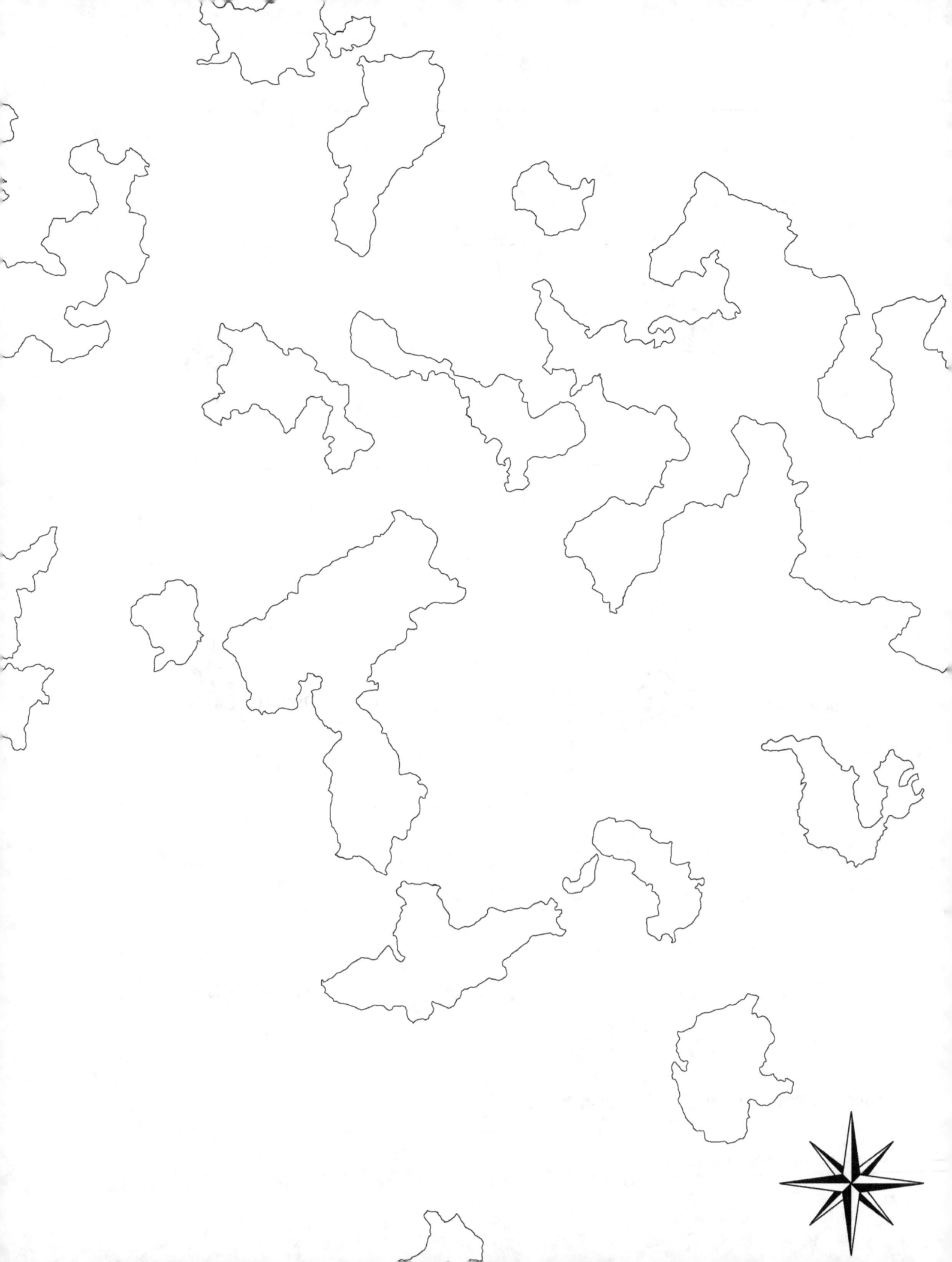

M A P

Story:

Cities

Landmarks

_____

_____

_____

_____

_____

Bodies of Water

Provinces/Districts

_____

_____

_____

_____

Lines and Symbols

Scale

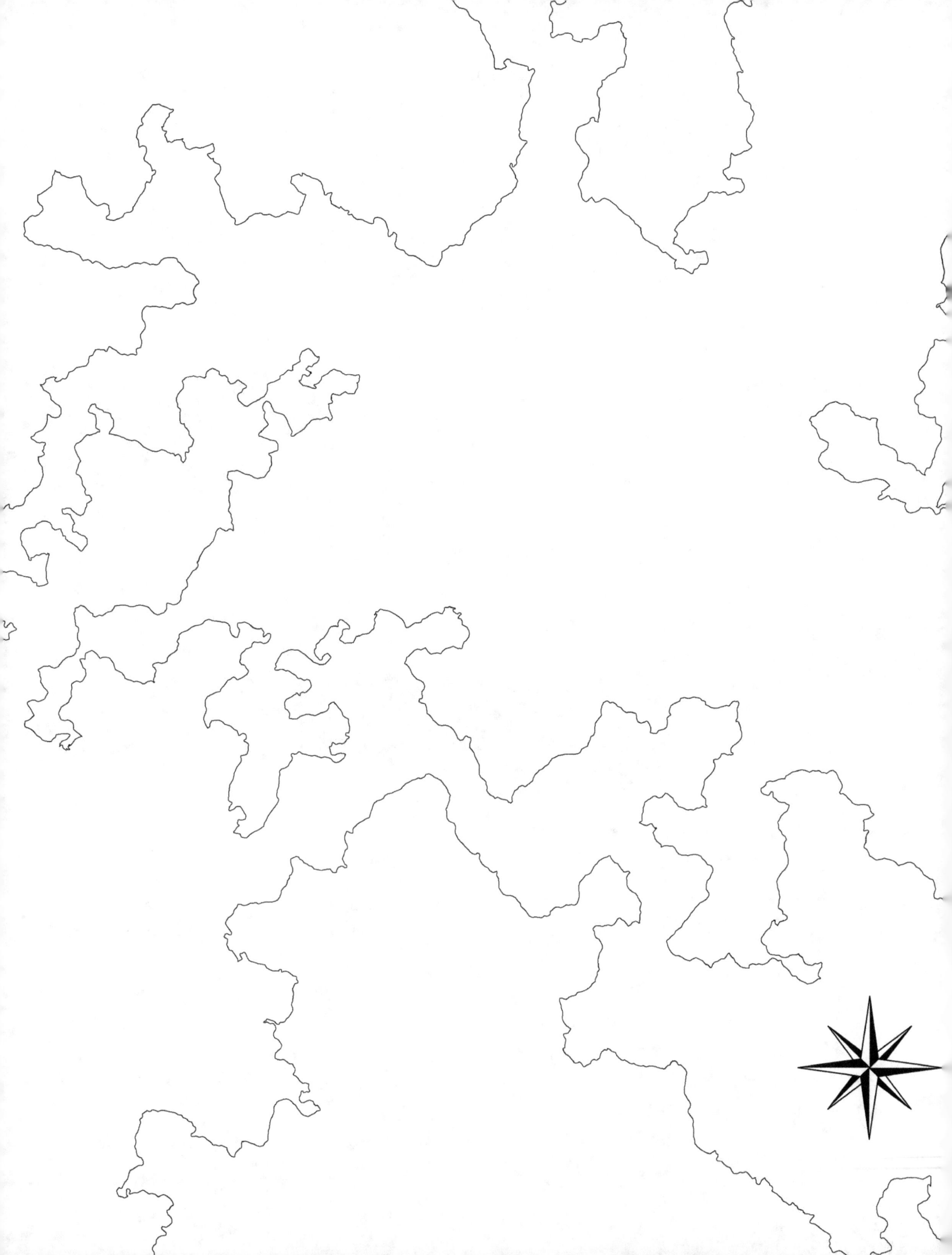

MAP

Story:

_____

Cities

_____
_____
_____
_____

Landmarks

_____
_____
_____
_____

Bodies of Water

_____
_____
_____
_____

Provinces/Districts

_____
_____
_____
_____

Lines and Symbols

Scale

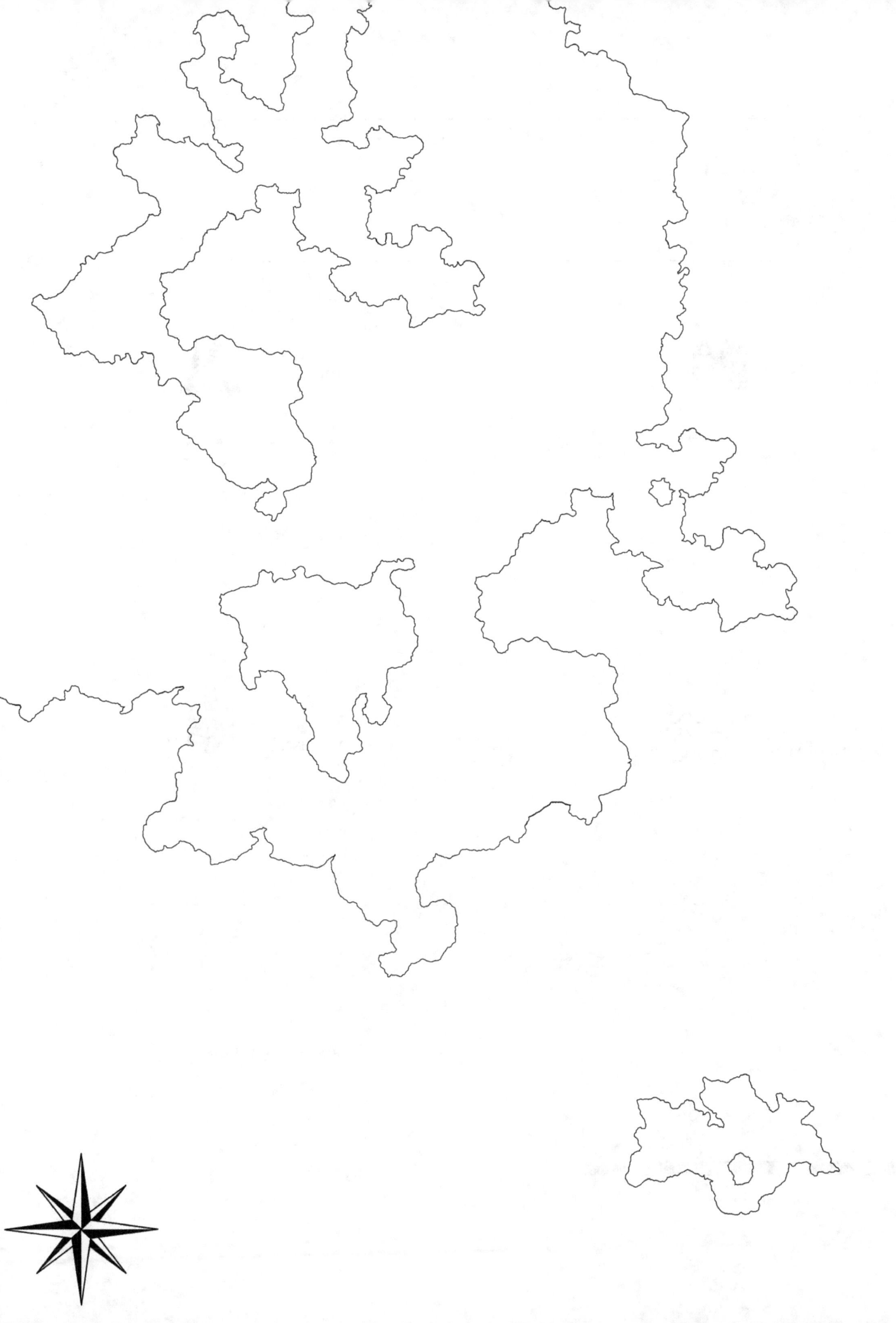

MAP

Story: _____

_____

Cities

Landmarks

_____
_____
_____
_____
_____

_____
_____
_____
_____
_____

Bodies of Water

Provinces/Districts

_____
_____
_____
_____

_____
_____
_____
_____

Lines and Symbols

Scale

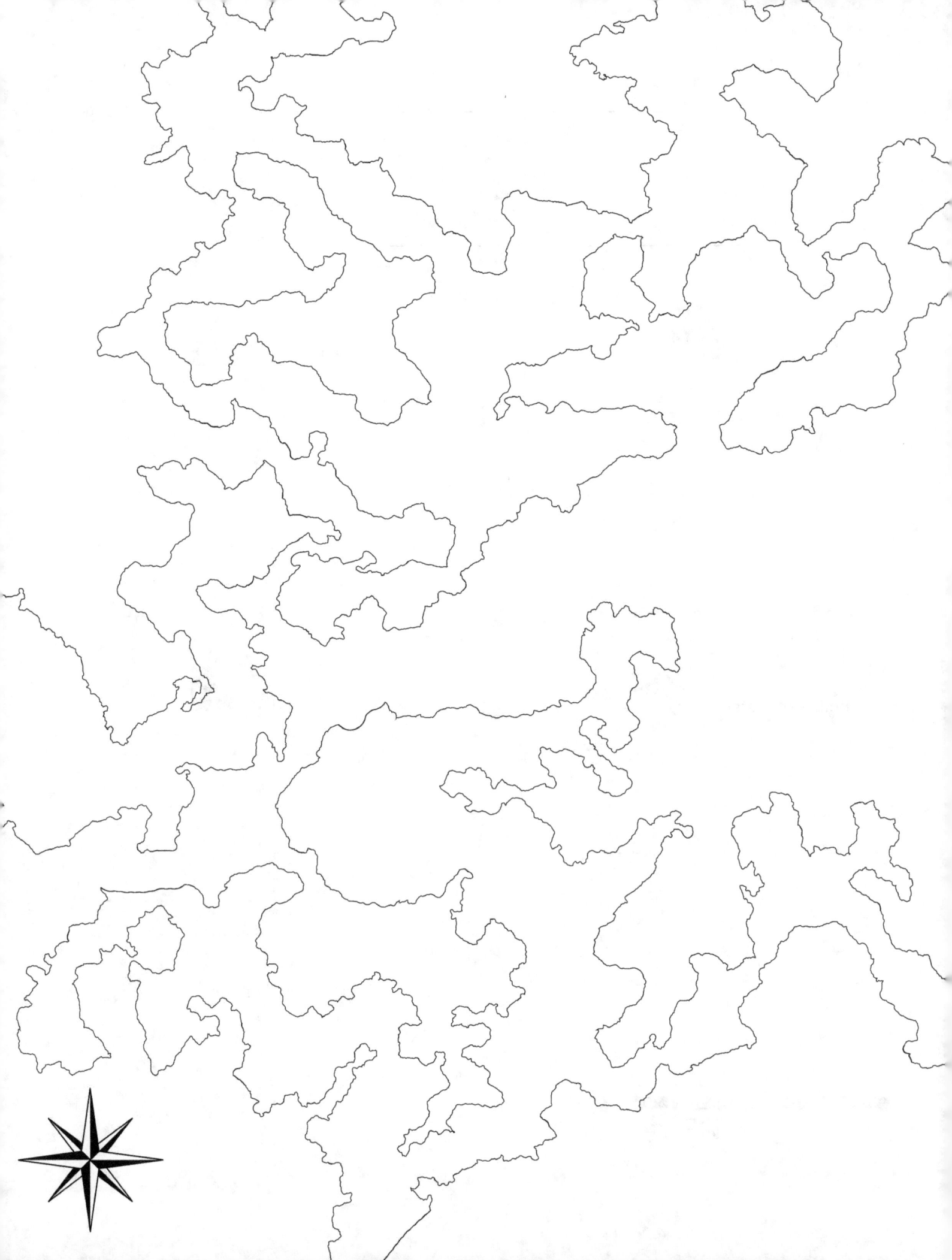

M A P

Story:

_____

Cities

Landmarks

Bodies of Water

Provinces/Districts

Lines and Symbols

Scale

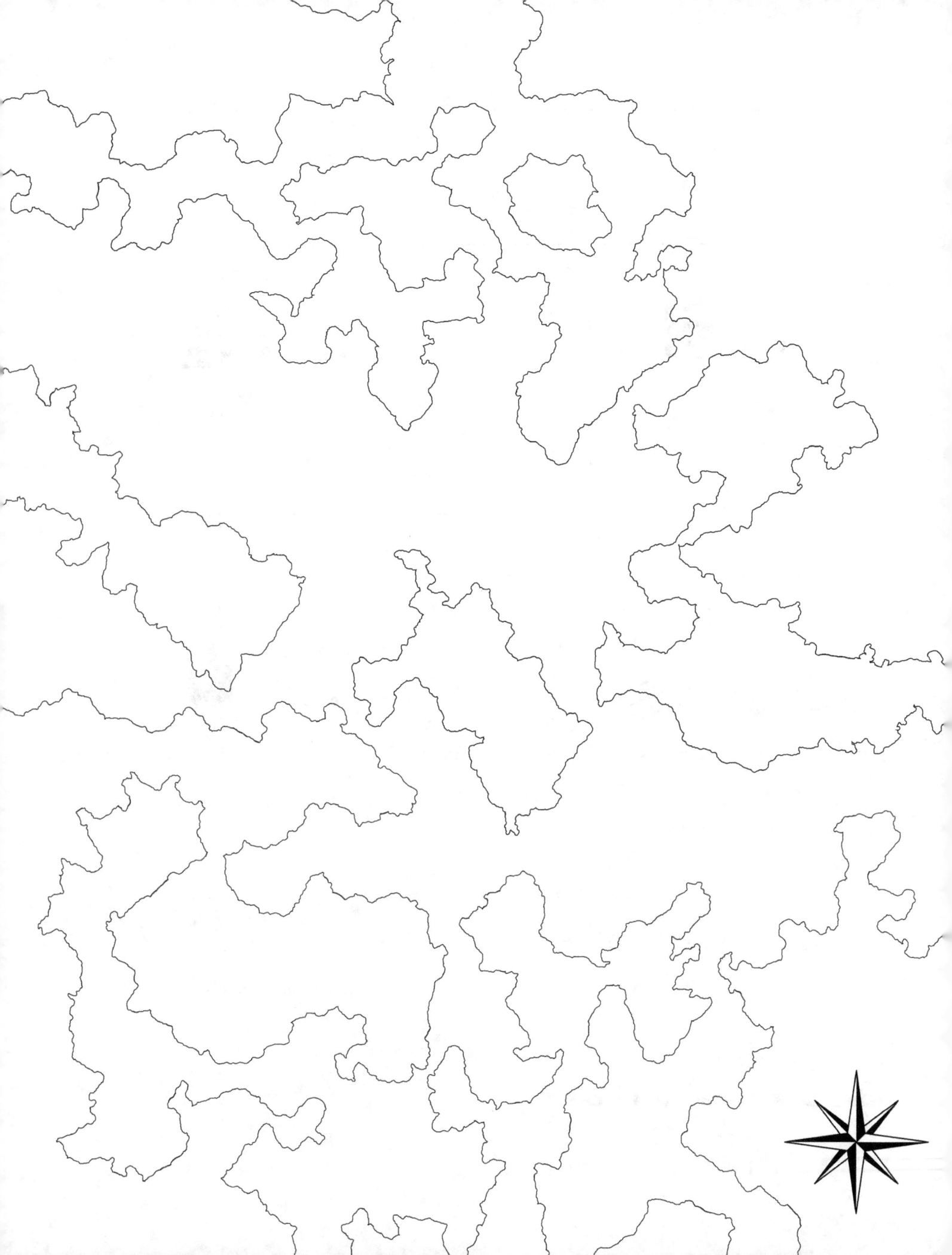

M A P

Story:

_____

Cities

_____
_____
_____
_____

Landmarks

_____
_____
_____
_____

Bodies of Water

_____
_____
_____
_____

Provinces/Districts

_____
_____
_____
_____

Lines and Symbols

Scale

30

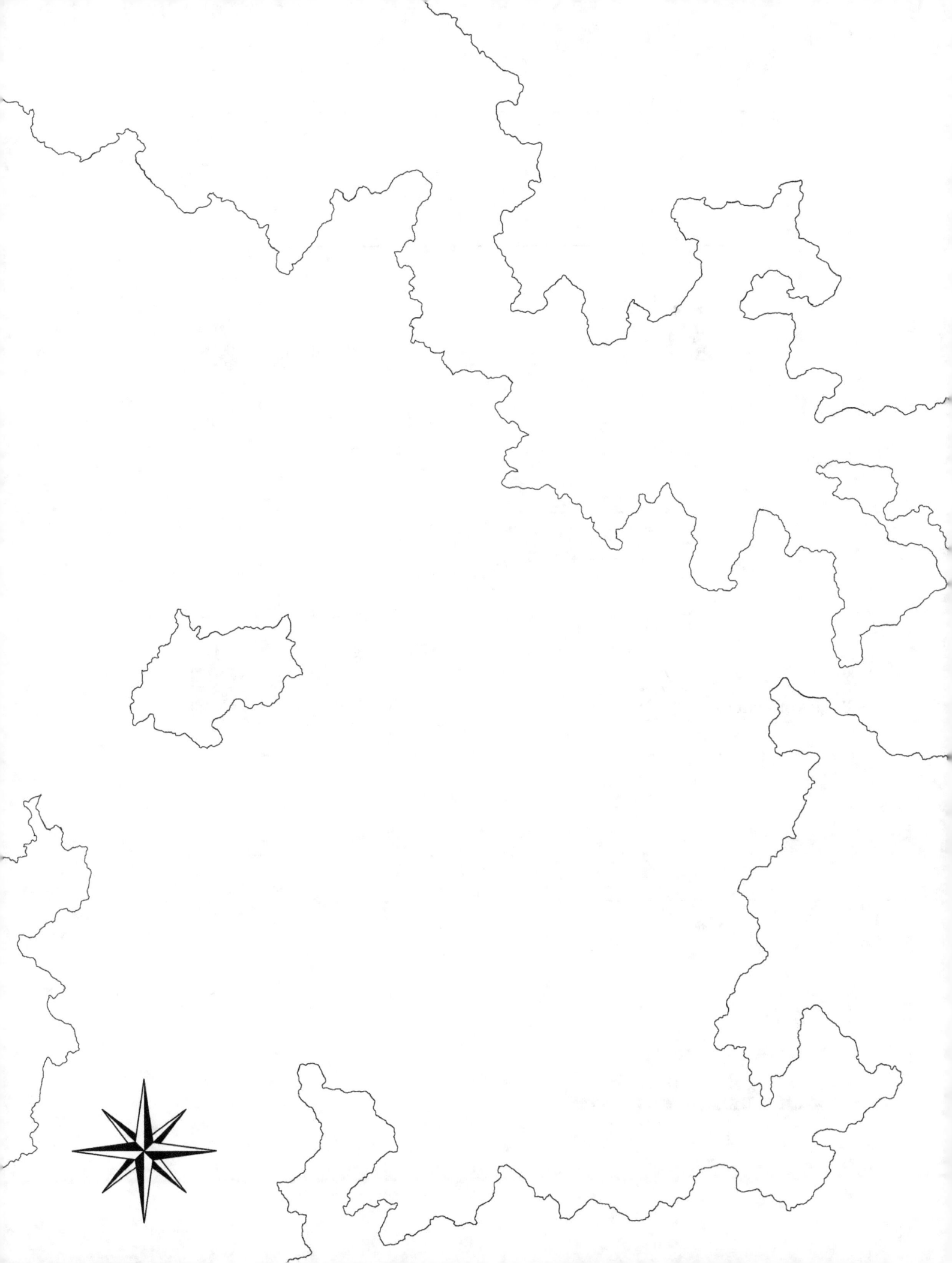

M A P

Story:

Cities

Landmarks

Bodies of Water

Provinces/Districts

Lines and Symbols

Scale

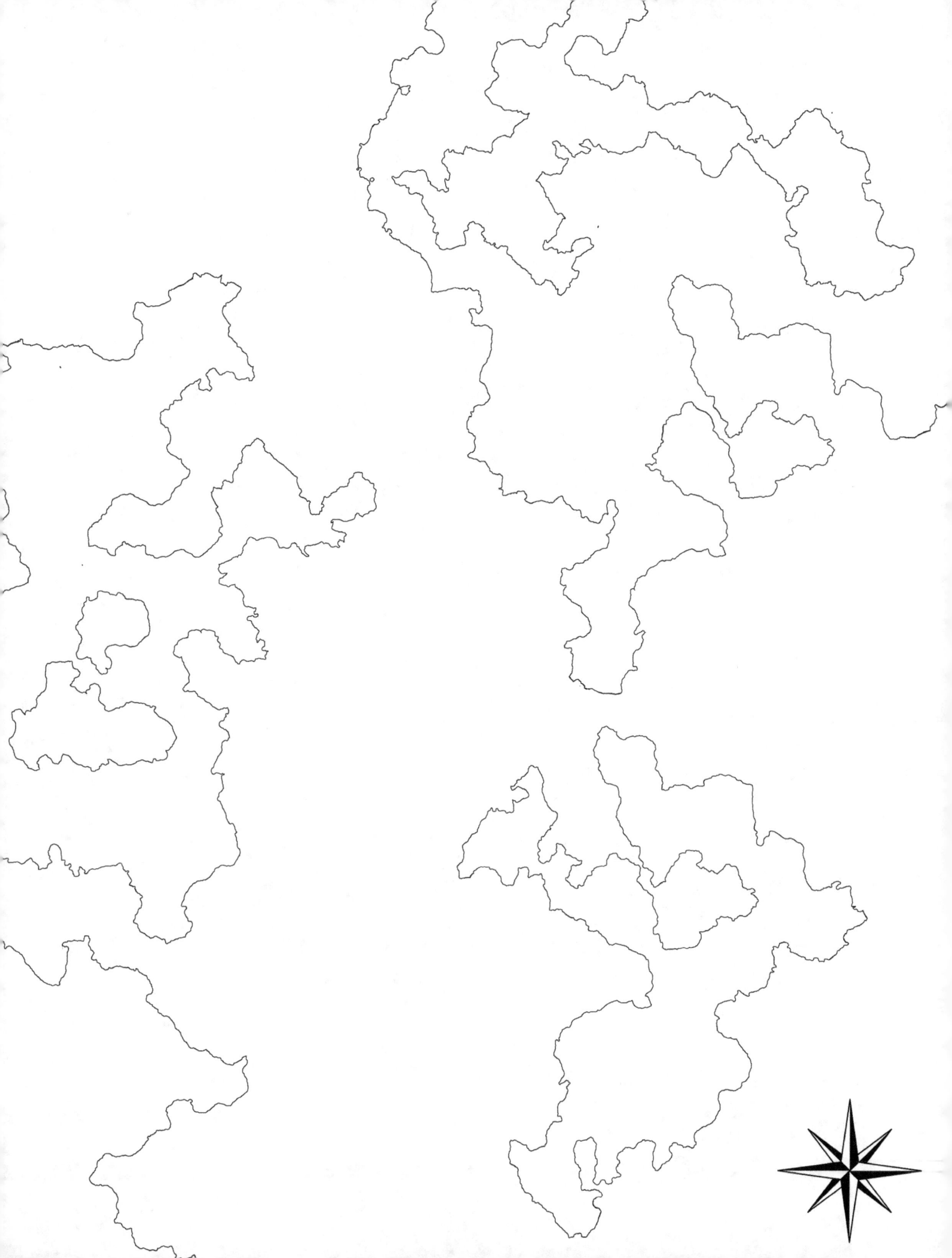

Planets

We all come from our own little planets. That's why we're all
different. That's what makes life interesting.

Robert E. Sherwood

M A P

Story:

_____

Cities

Landmarks

Bodies of Water

Provinces/Districts

Lines and Symbols

Scale

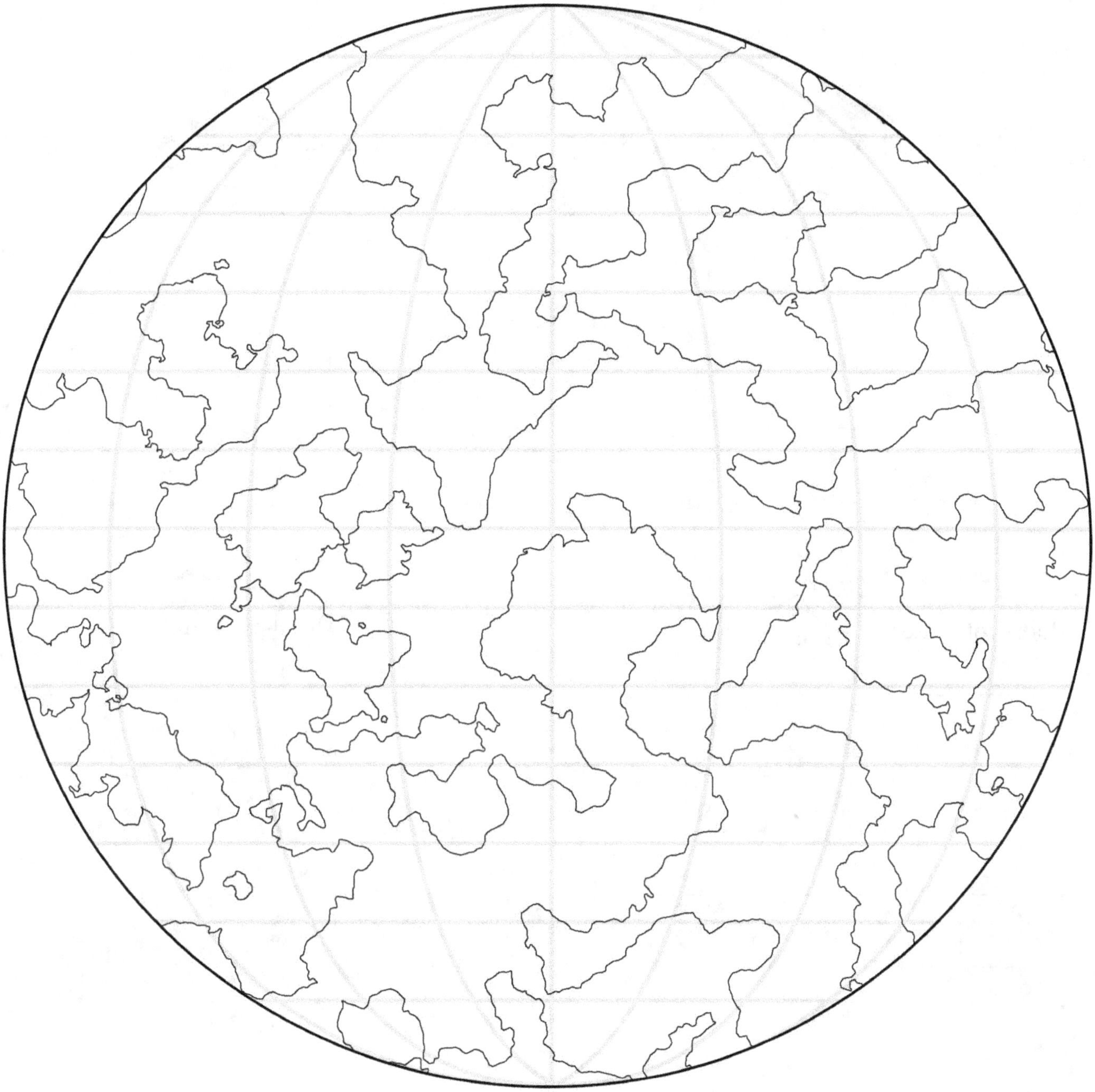

M A P

Story:

_____

Cities

Landmarks

Bodies of Water

Provinces/Districts

Lines and Symbols

Scale

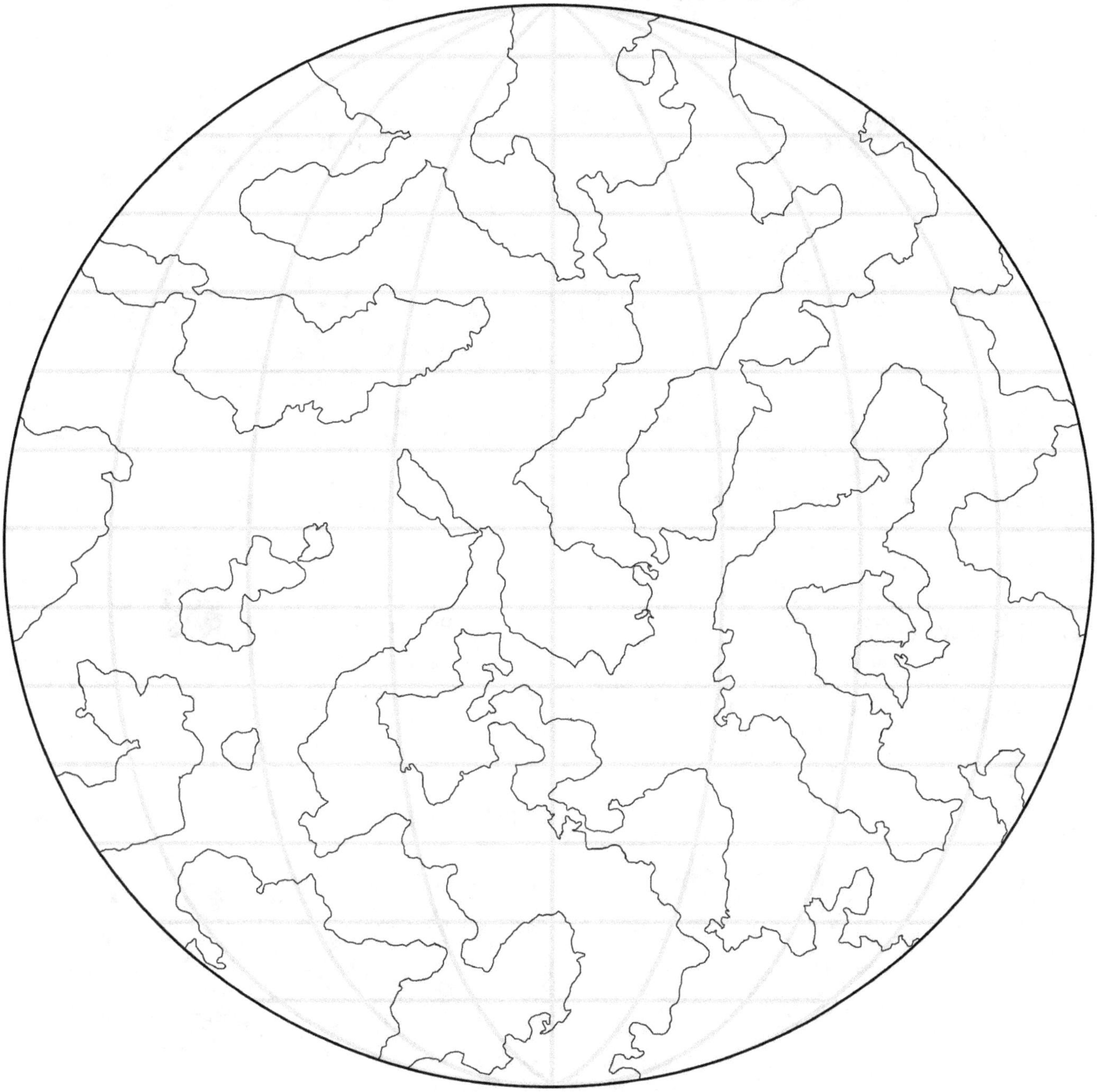

M A P

Story:

_____

Cities

_____
_____
_____
_____
_____

Landmarks

_____
_____
_____
_____
_____

Bodies of Water

_____
_____
_____
_____
_____

Provinces/Districts

_____
_____
_____
_____
_____

Lines and Symbols

Scale

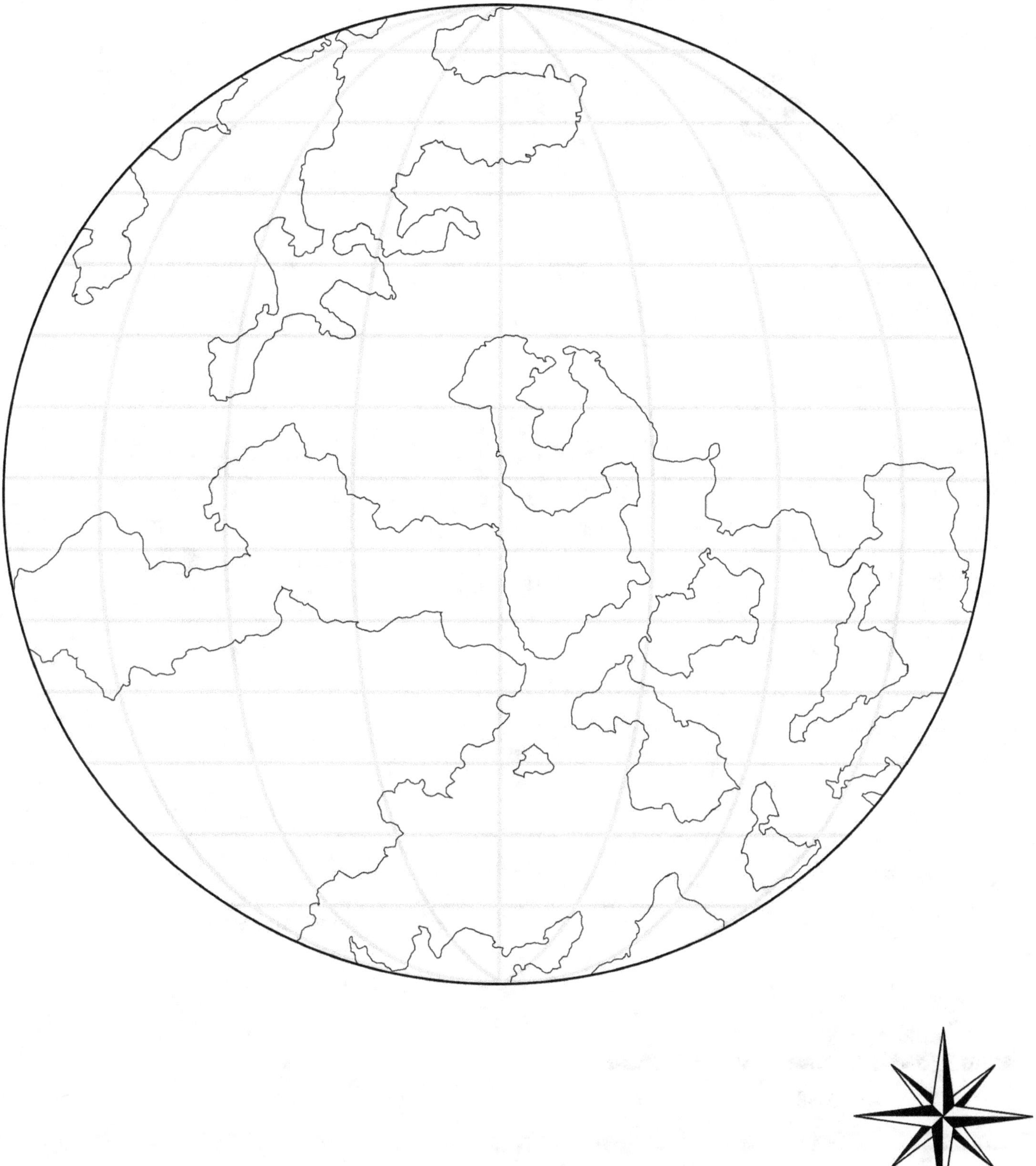

M A P

Story:

_____

Cities

Landmarks

_____
_____
_____
_____
_____

_____
_____
_____
_____
_____

Bodies of Water

Provinces/Districts

_____
_____
_____
_____
_____

_____
_____
_____
_____
_____

Lines and Symbols

Scale

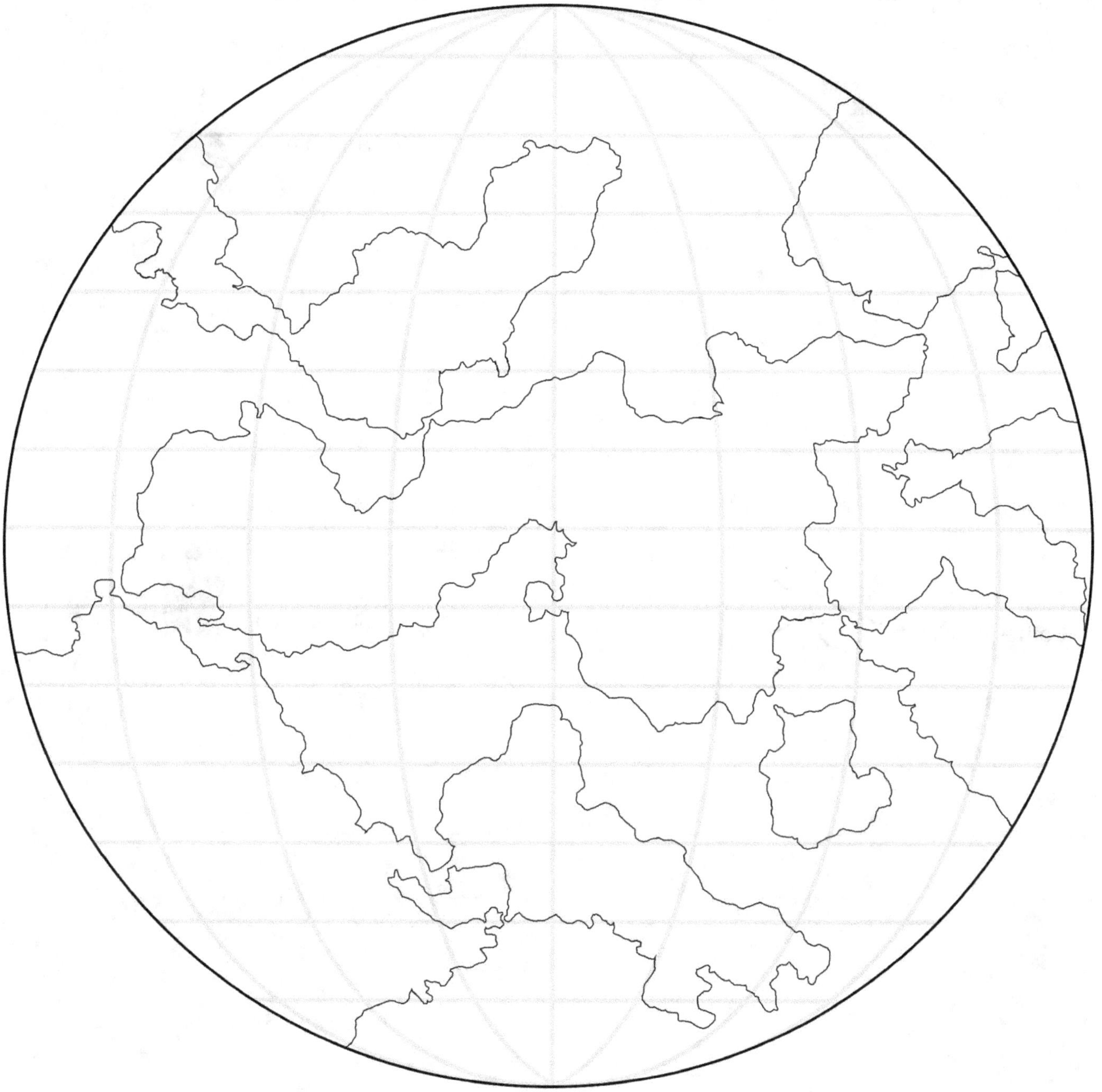

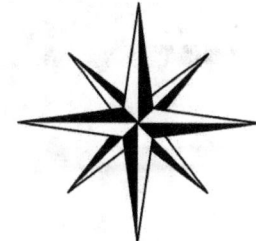

MAP

Story: _____

Cities

_____
_____
_____
_____

Landmarks

_____
_____
_____
_____

Bodies of Water

_____
_____
_____
_____

Provinces/Districts

_____
_____
_____
_____

Lines and Symbols

Scale

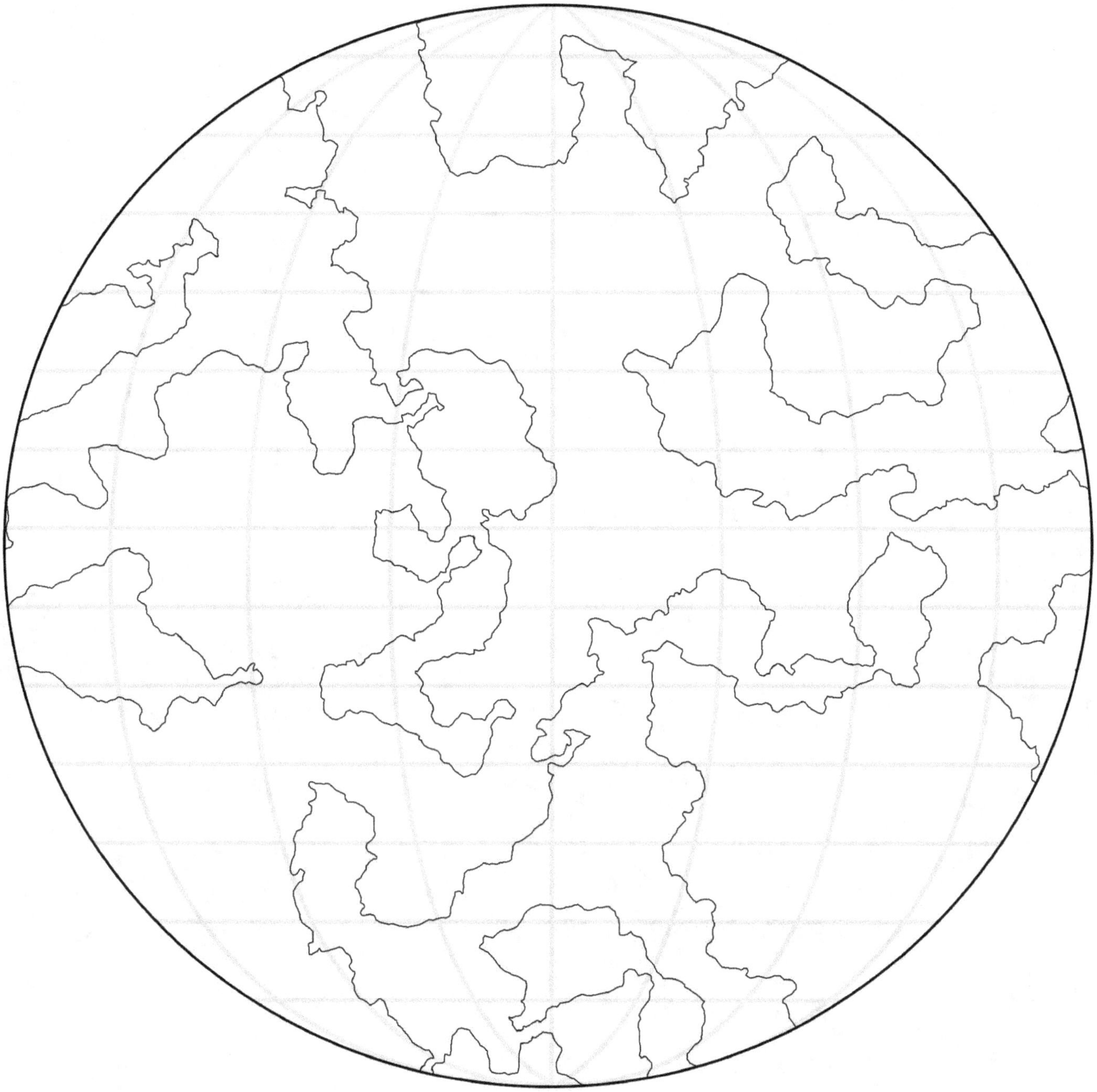

MAP

Story:

_____

Cities

Landmarks

_____
_____
_____
_____
_____

Bodies of Water

Provinces/Districts

_____
_____
_____
_____

Lines and Symbols

Scale

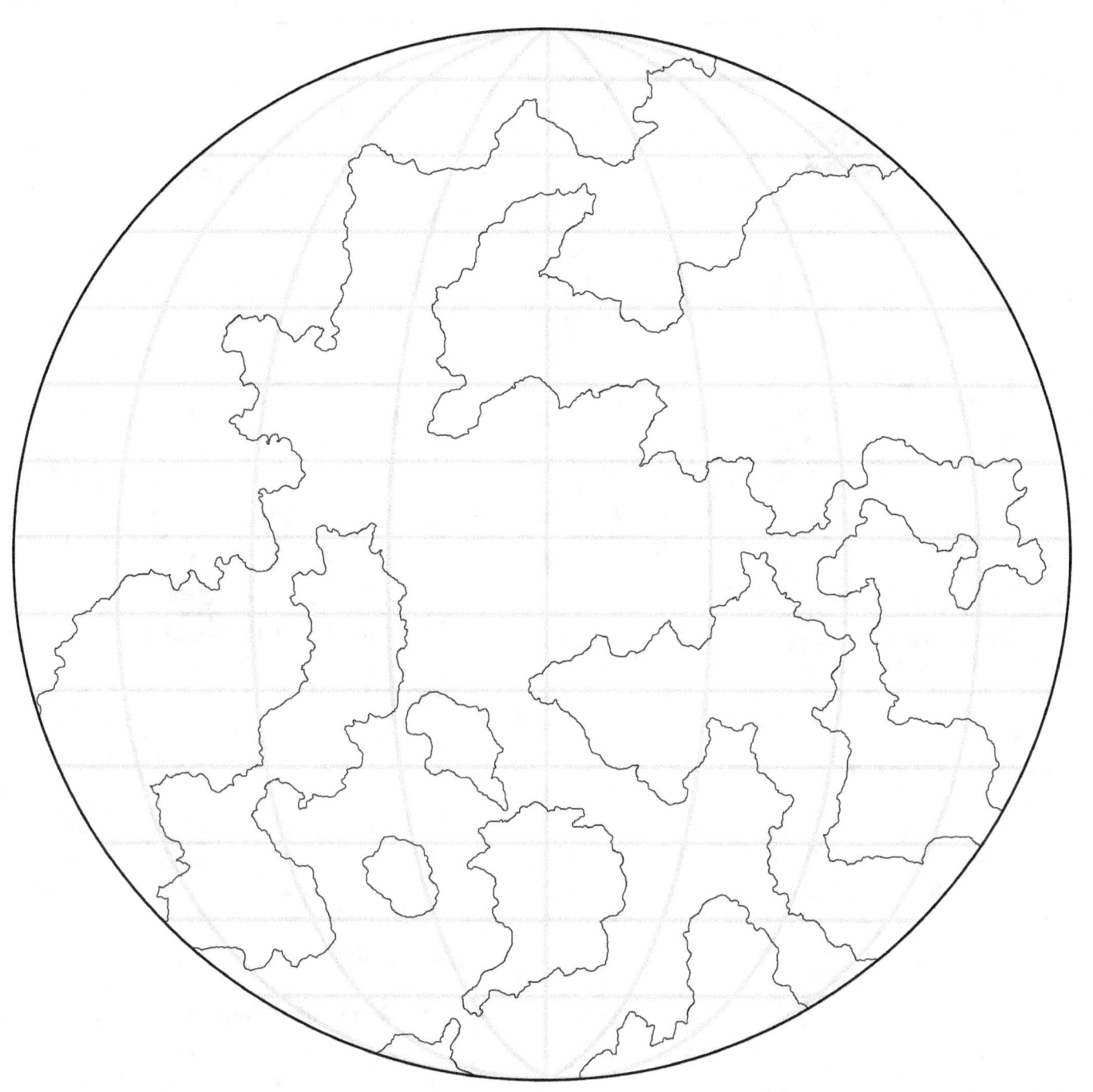

MAP

Story:

_____

Cities

_____
_____
_____
_____

Landmarks

_____
_____
_____
_____

Bodies of Water

_____
_____
_____
_____

Provinces/Districts

_____
_____
_____
_____

Lines and Symbols

Scale

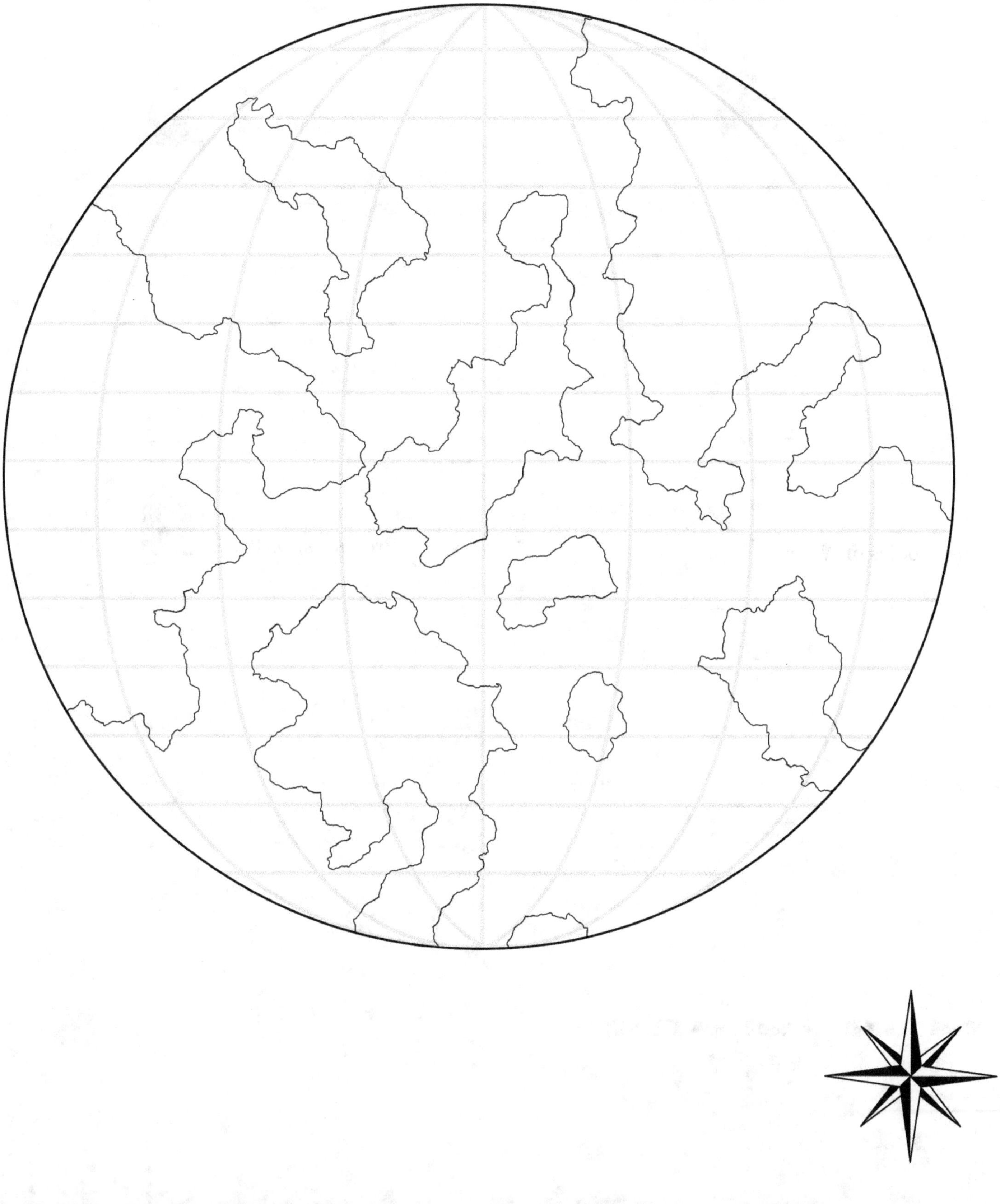

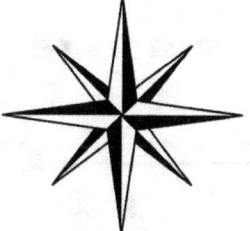

M A P

Story:

Cities

Landmarks

Bodies of Water

Provinces/Districts

Lines and Symbols

Scale

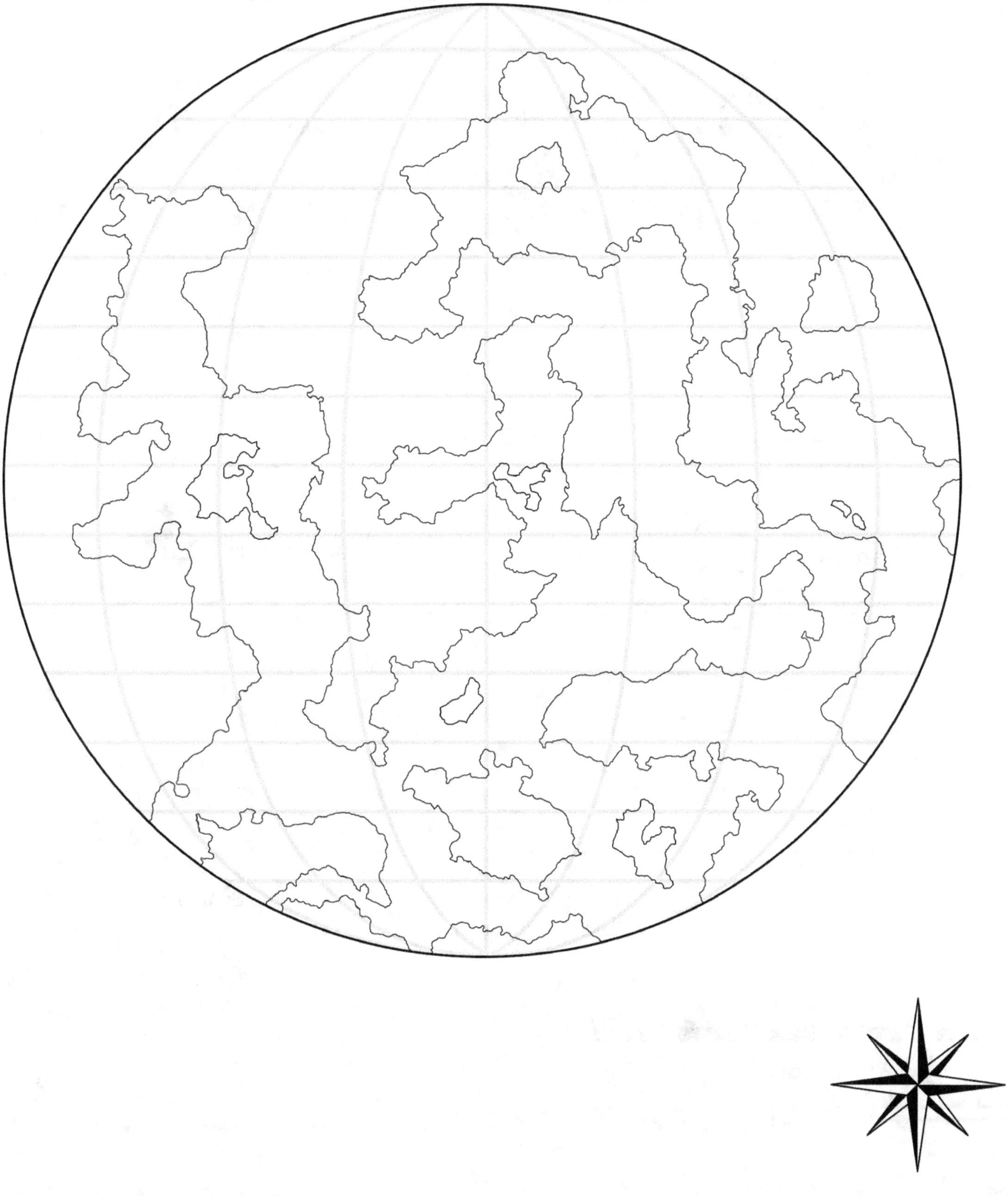

M A P

Story:

_____

Cities

Landmarks

Bodies of Water

Provinces/Districts

Lines and Symbols

Scale

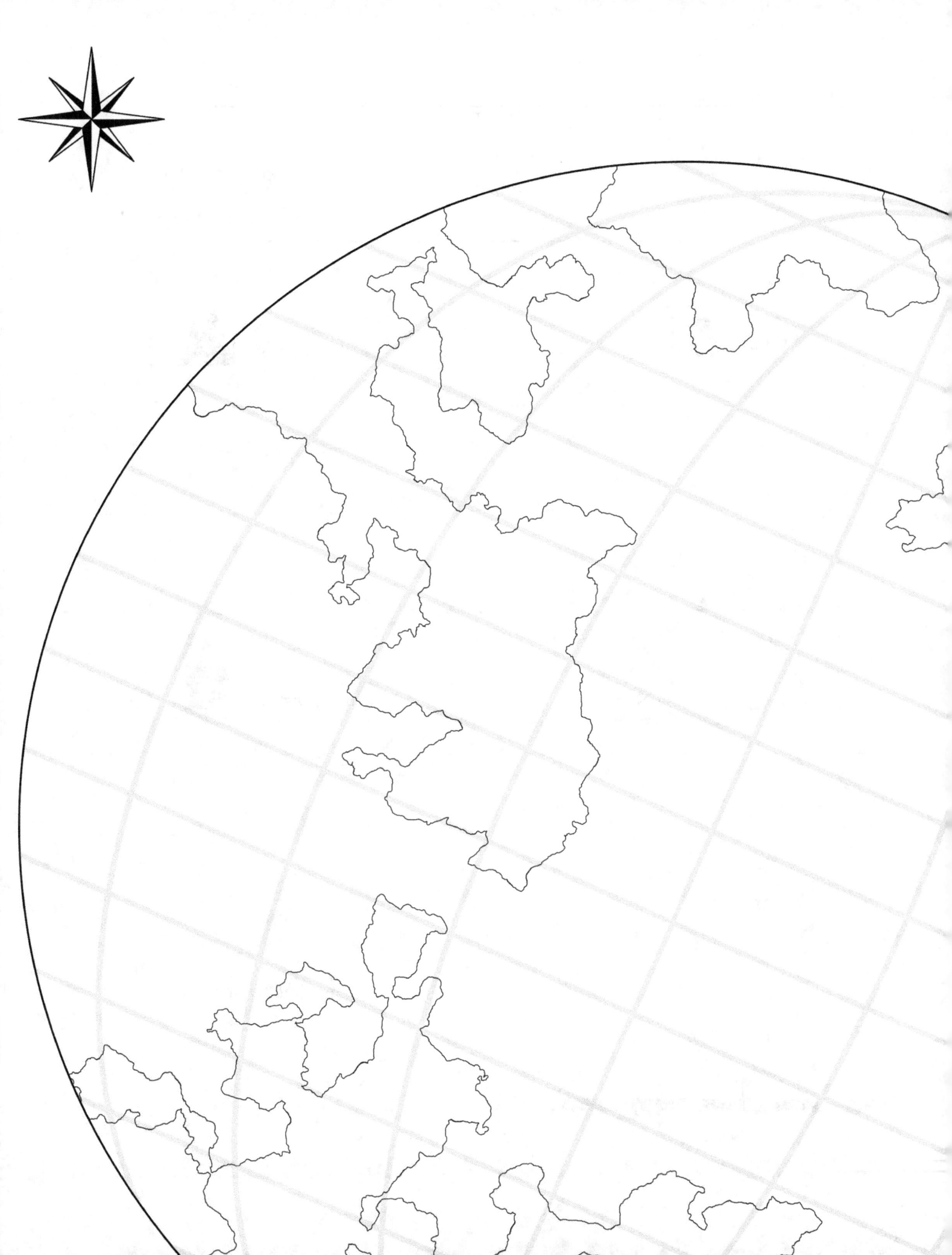

M A P

Story:

_____

Cities

Landmarks

Bodies of Water

Provinces/Districts

Lines and Symbols

Scale

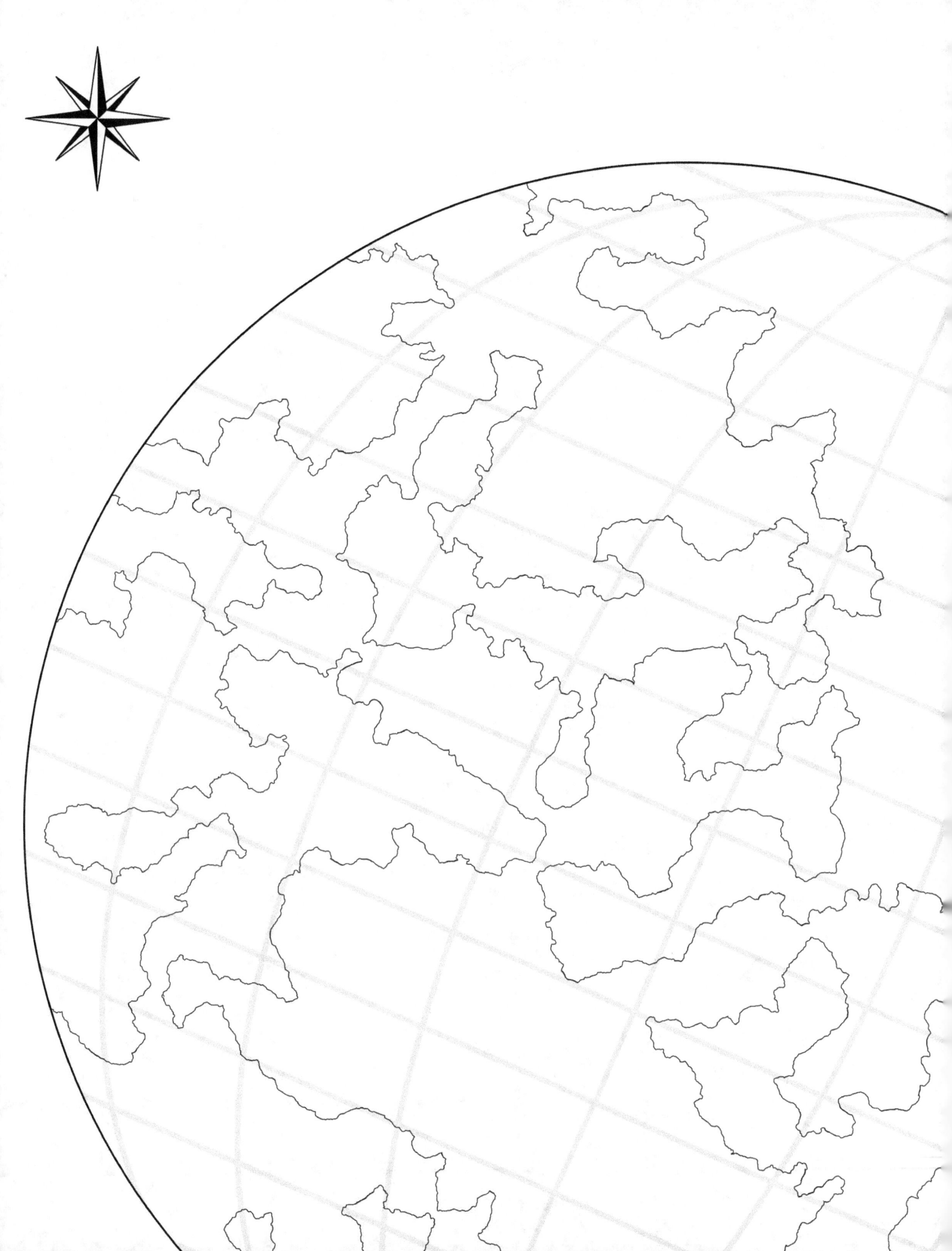

Islands

Islands intrigue me. You can see the perimeters of your world.
It's a microcosm.

Jamie Wyeth

M A P

Story: _____

_____

Cities

_____
_____
_____
_____

Landmarks

_____
_____
_____
_____

Bodies of Water

_____
_____
_____
_____

Provinces/Districts

_____
_____
_____
_____

Lines and Symbols

Scale

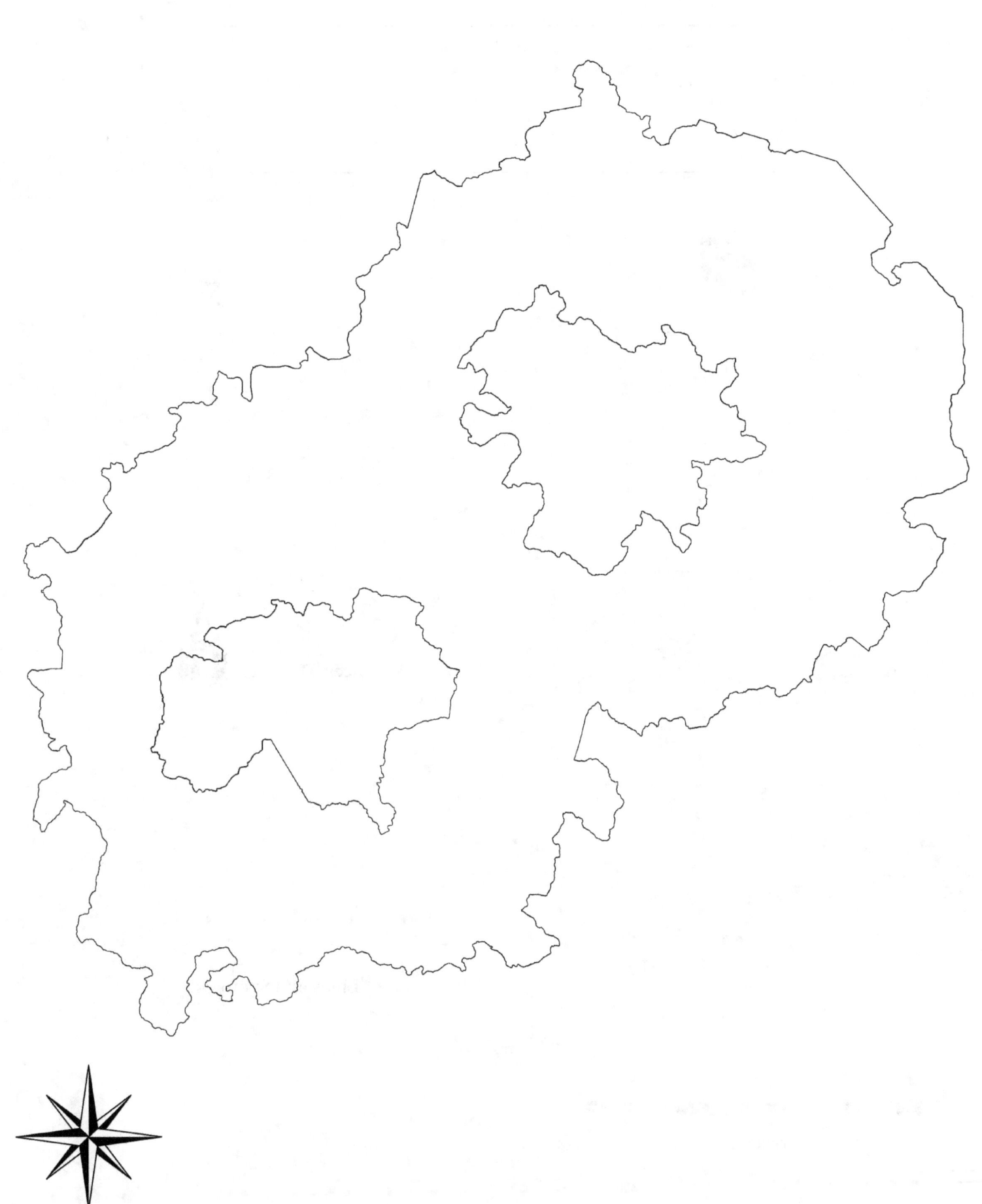

M A P

Story:

_____

Cities

_____

_____

_____

_____

_____

Landmarks

_____

_____

_____

_____

_____

Bodies of Water

_____

_____

_____

_____

Provinces/Districts

_____

_____

_____

_____

Lines and Symbols

Scale

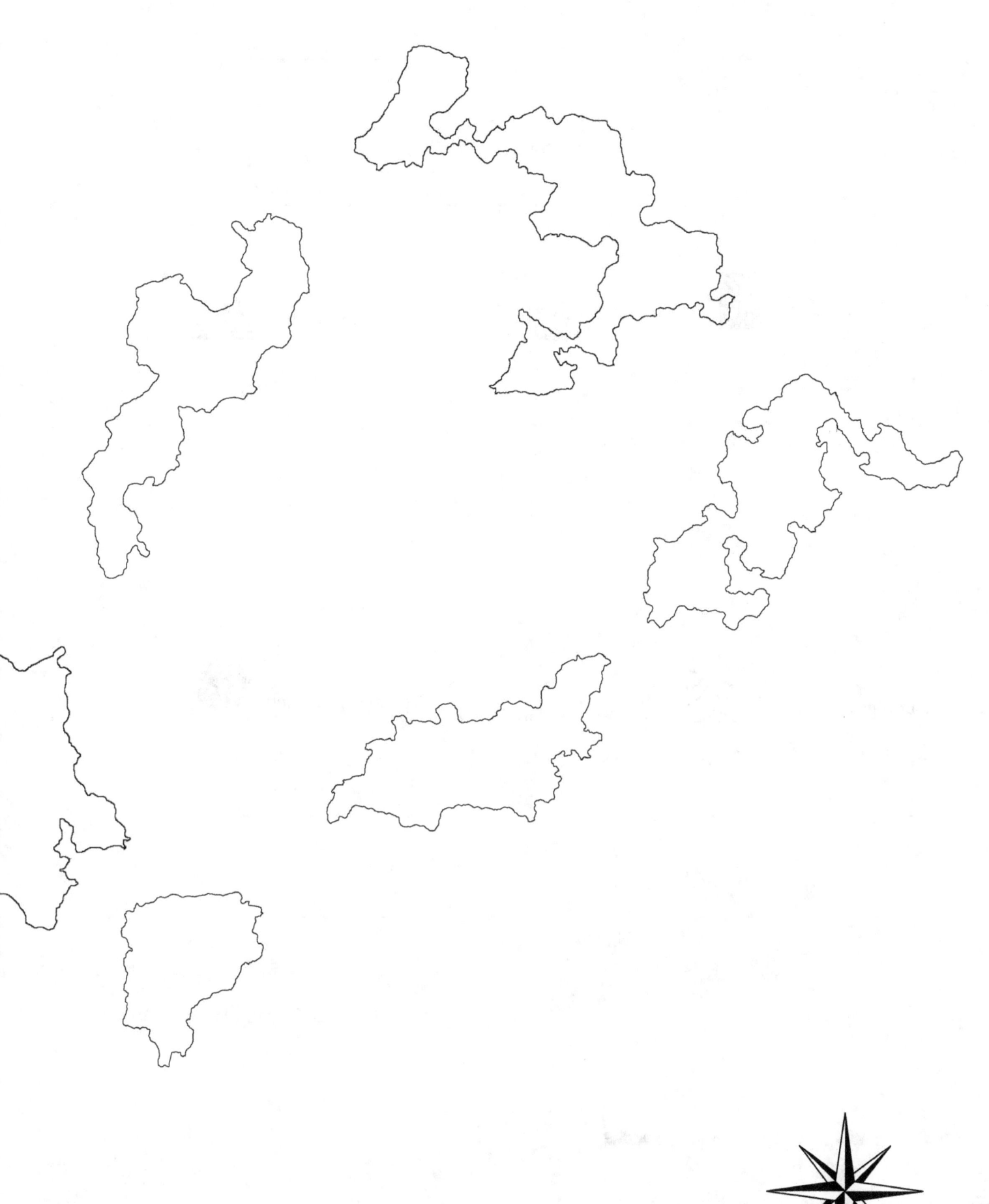

MAP

Story:

Cities

Landmarks

Bodies of Water

Provinces/Districts

Lines and Symbols

Scale

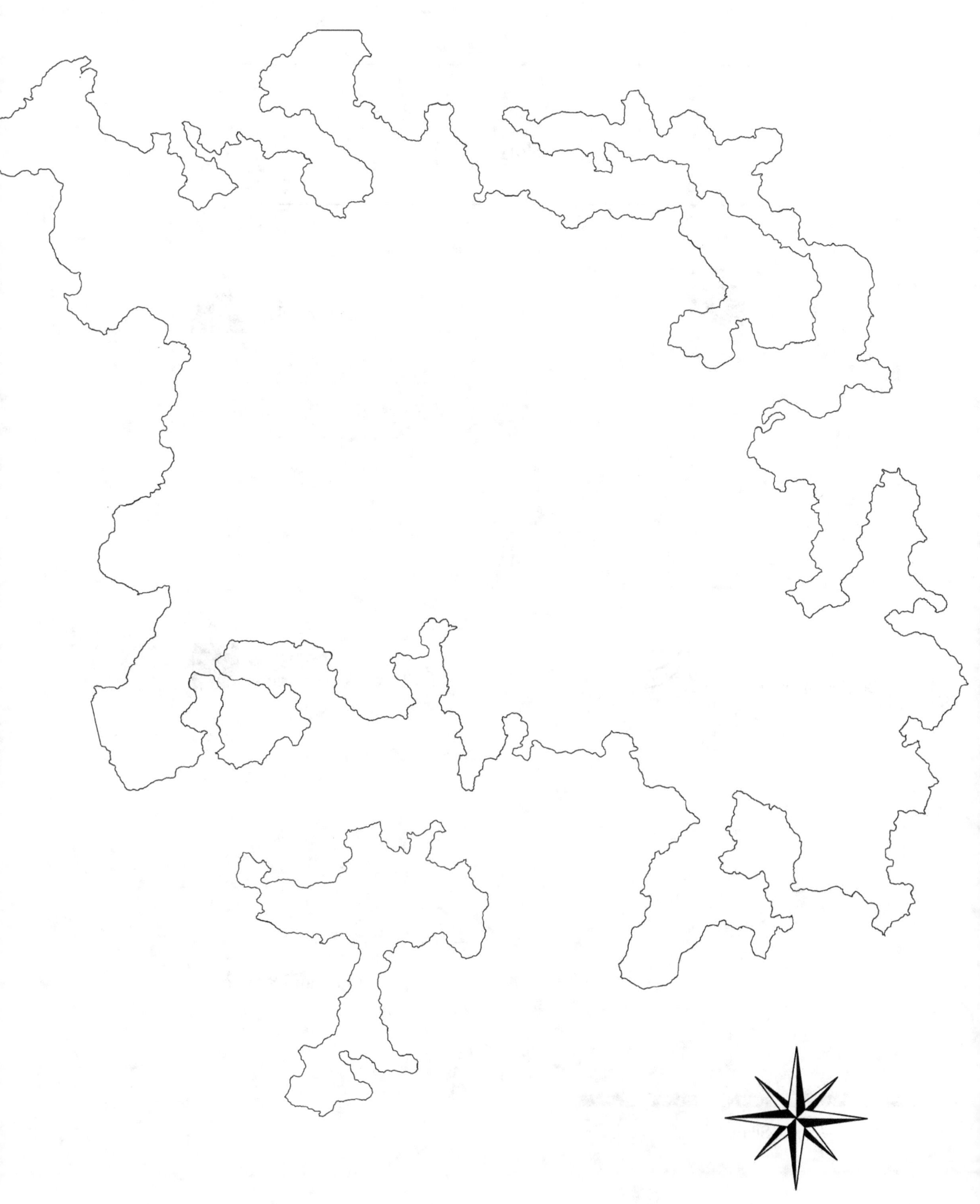

M A P

Story:

_____

Cities

Landmarks

Bodies of Water

Provinces/Districts

Lines and Symbols

Scale

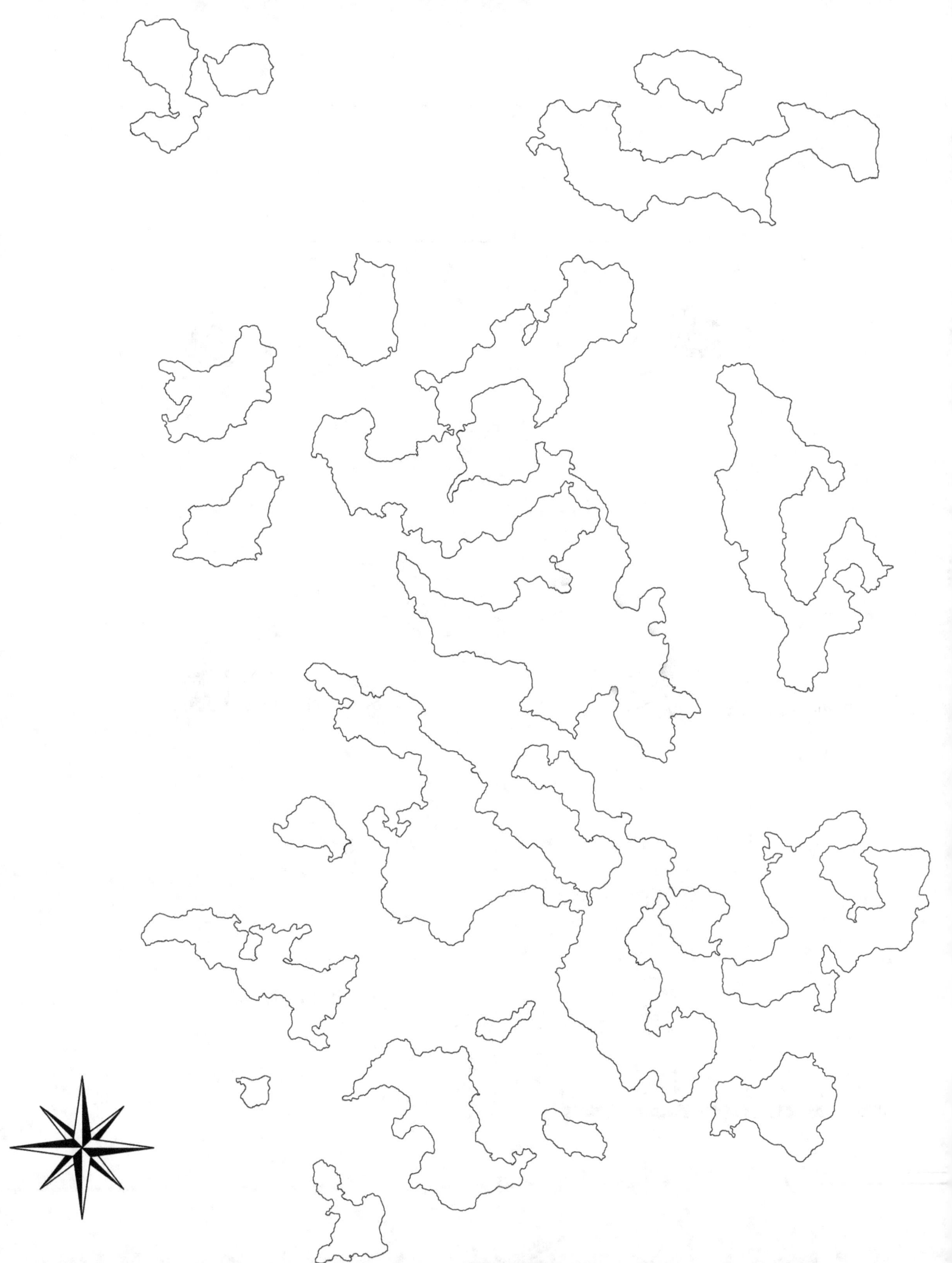

MAP

Story:

_____

Cities

Landmarks

Bodies of Water

Provinces/Districts

Lines and Symbols

Scale

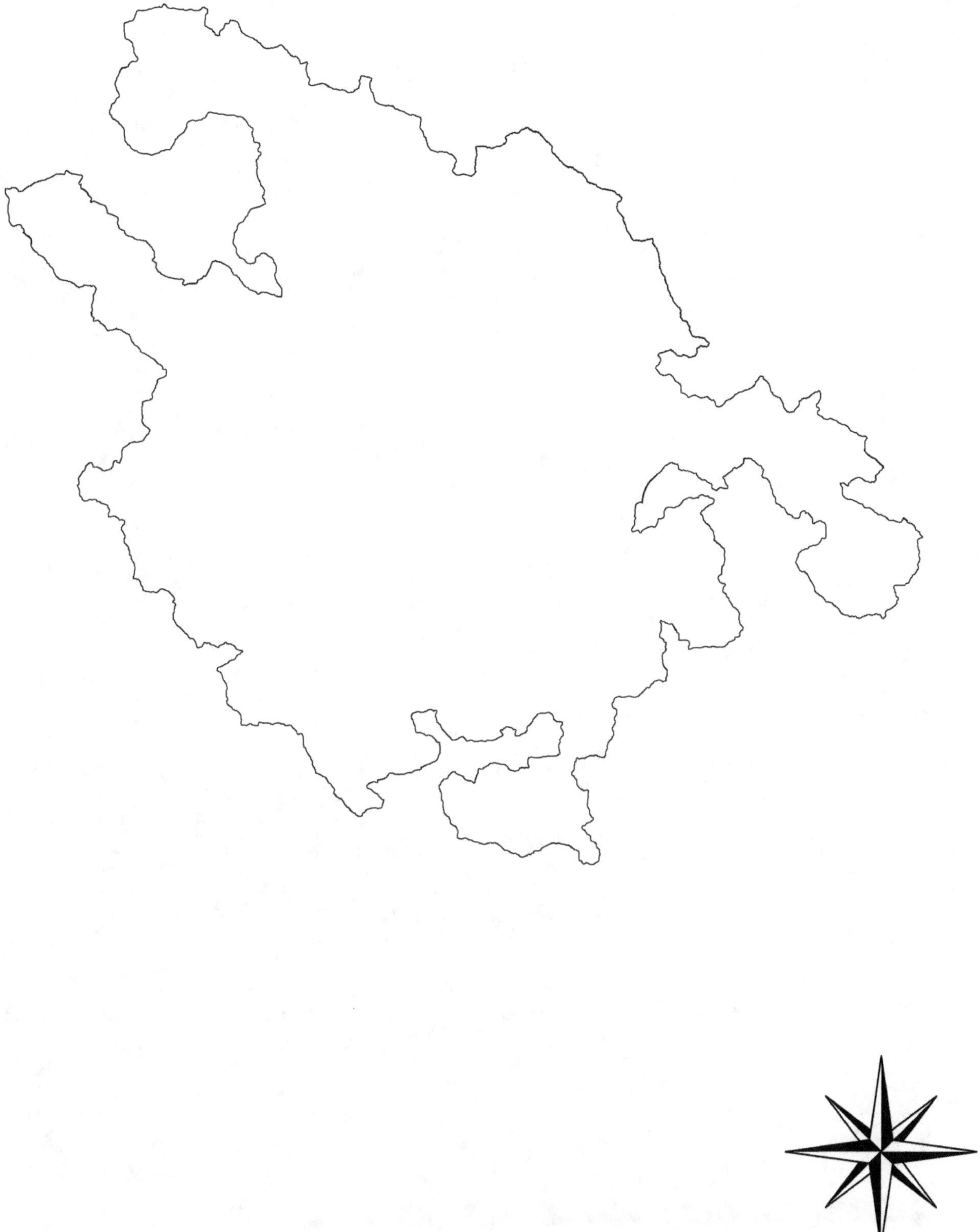

MAP

Story: _____

_____

Cities

Landmarks

_____
_____
_____
_____
_____

_____
_____
_____
_____
_____

Bodies of Water

Provinces/Districts

_____
_____
_____
_____
_____

_____
_____
_____
_____
_____

Lines and Symbols

Scale

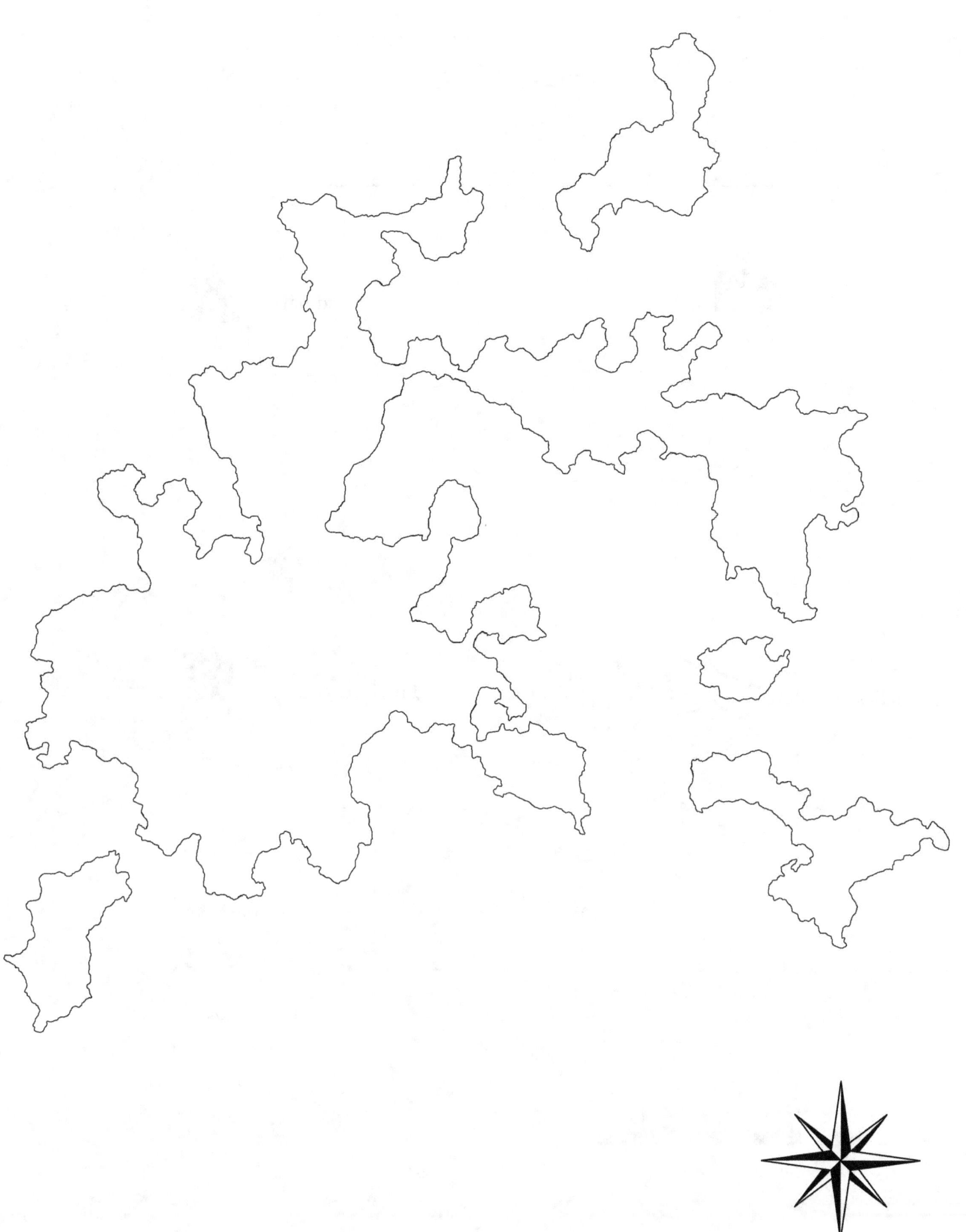

M A P

Story:

_____

Cities

Landmarks

_____
_____
_____
_____

_____
_____
_____
_____

Bodies of Water

Provinces/Districts

_____
_____
_____
_____

_____
_____
_____
_____

Lines and Symbols

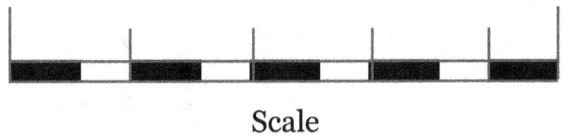

Scale

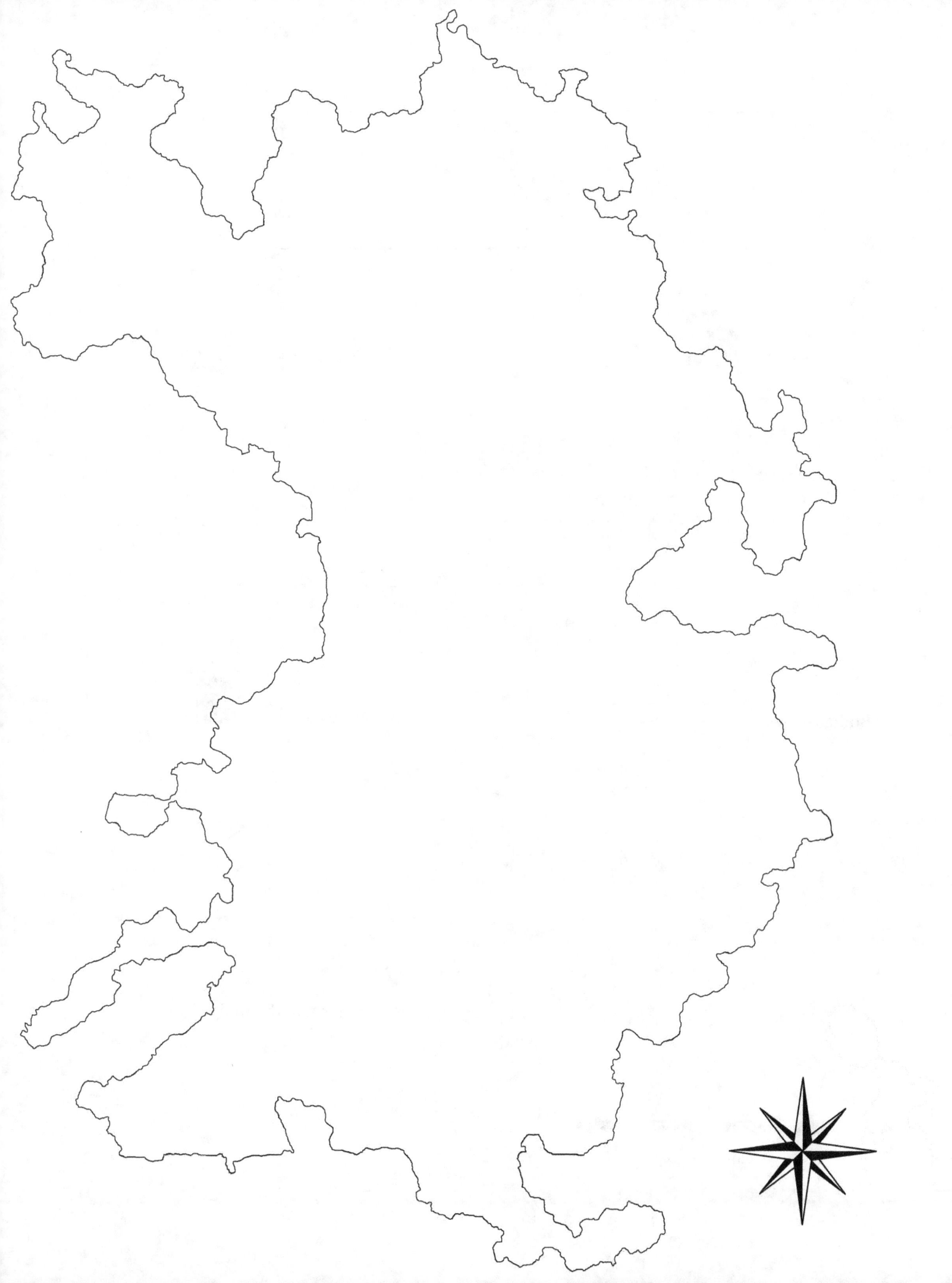

MAP

Story:

_____

Cities

_____
_____
_____
_____
_____

Landmarks

_____
_____
_____
_____
_____

Bodies of Water

_____
_____
_____
_____

Provinces/Districts

_____
_____
_____
_____

Lines and Symbols

Scale

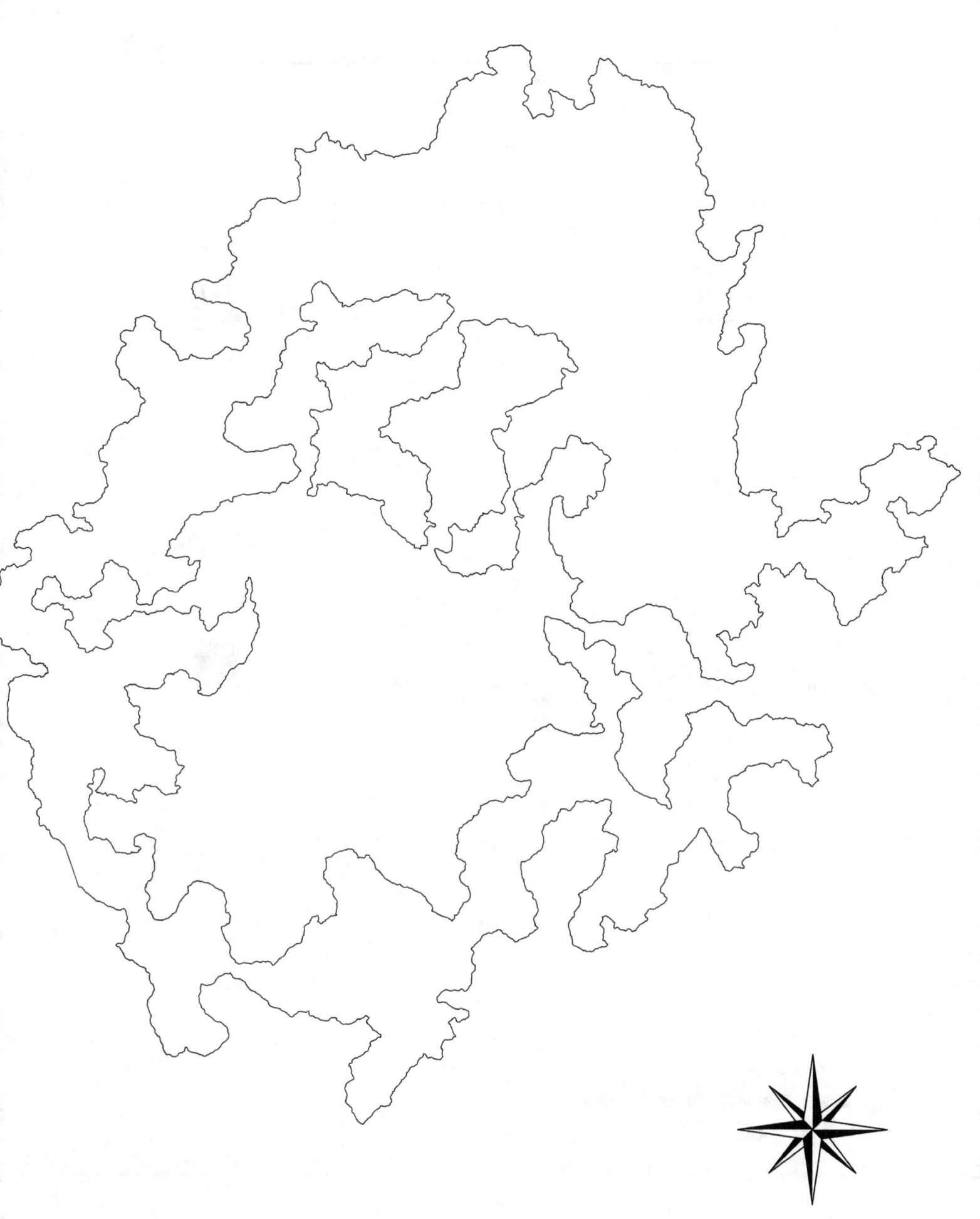

M A P

Story:

_____

Cities

_____
_____
_____
_____
_____

Landmarks

_____
_____
_____
_____
_____

Bodies of Water

_____
_____
_____
_____
_____

Provinces/Districts

_____
_____
_____
_____
_____

Lines and Symbols

Scale

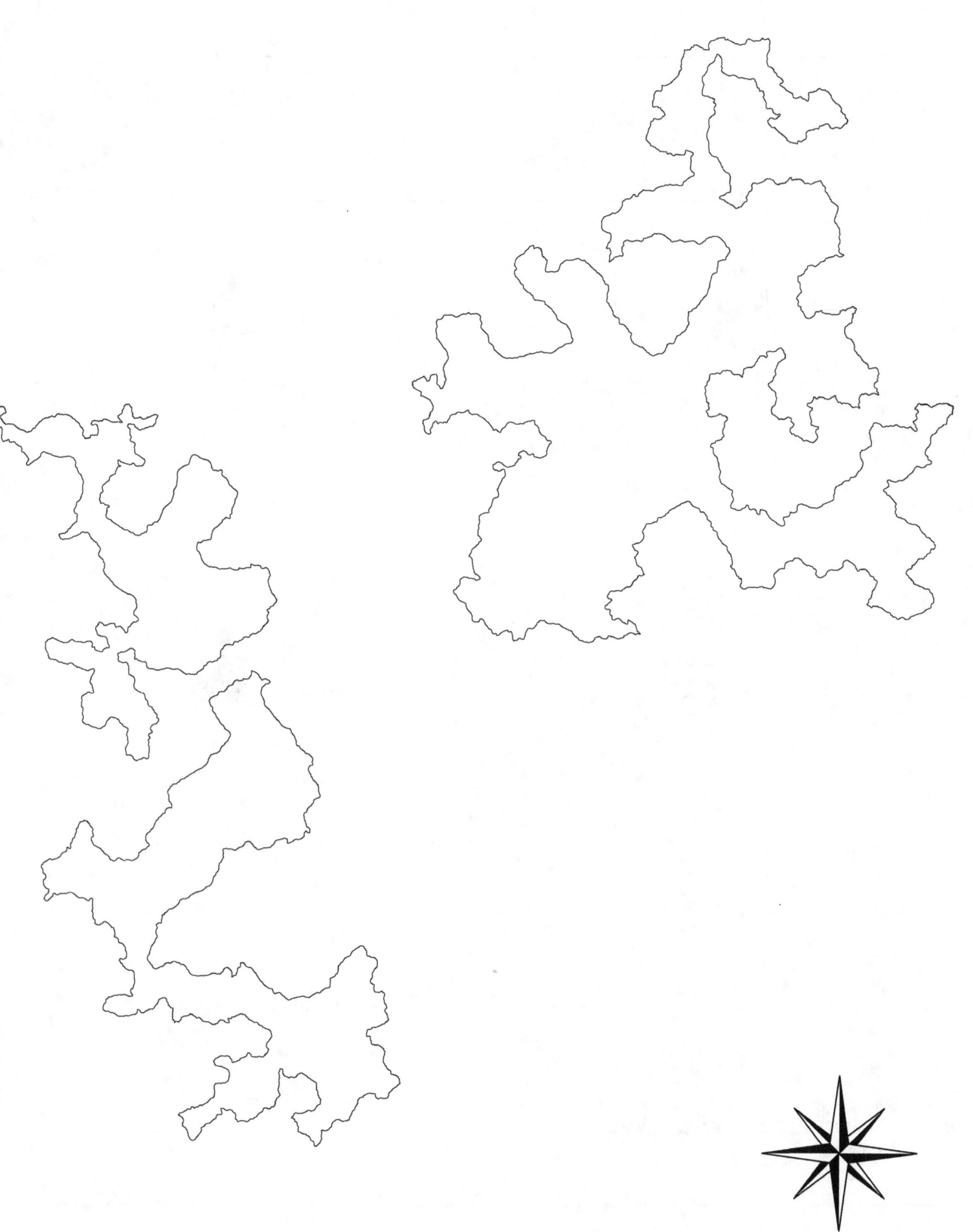

M A P

Story:

Cities

Landmarks

Bodies of Water

Provinces/Districts

Lines and Symbols

Scale

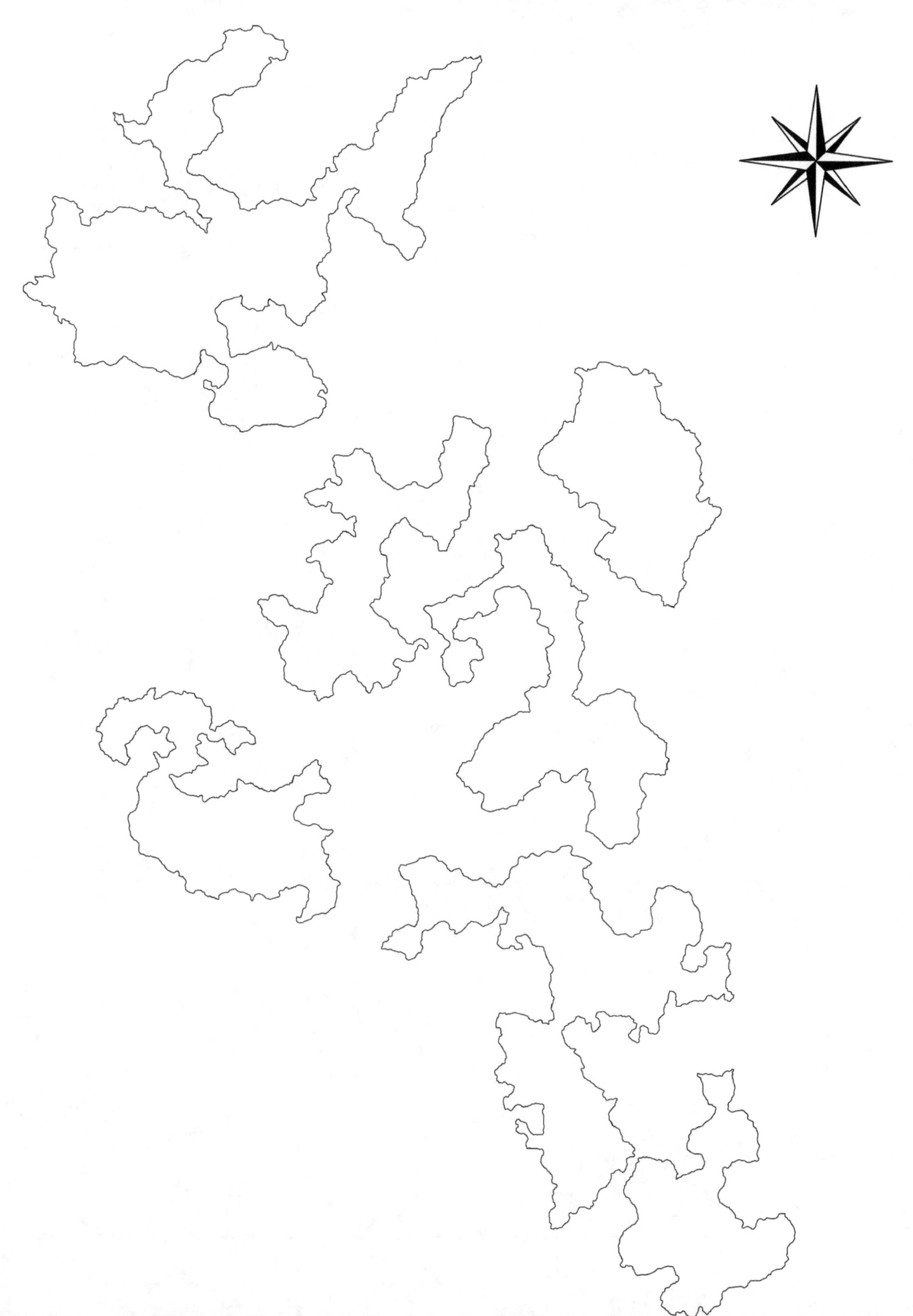

Cities & Towns

I have never felt salvation in nature. I love cities above all.

Michelangelo

MAP

Story: _____

_____

Houses

Landmarks

_____
_____
_____
_____
_____
_____

Town/Neighborhood

_____
_____
_____
_____

Scale

Lines and Symbols

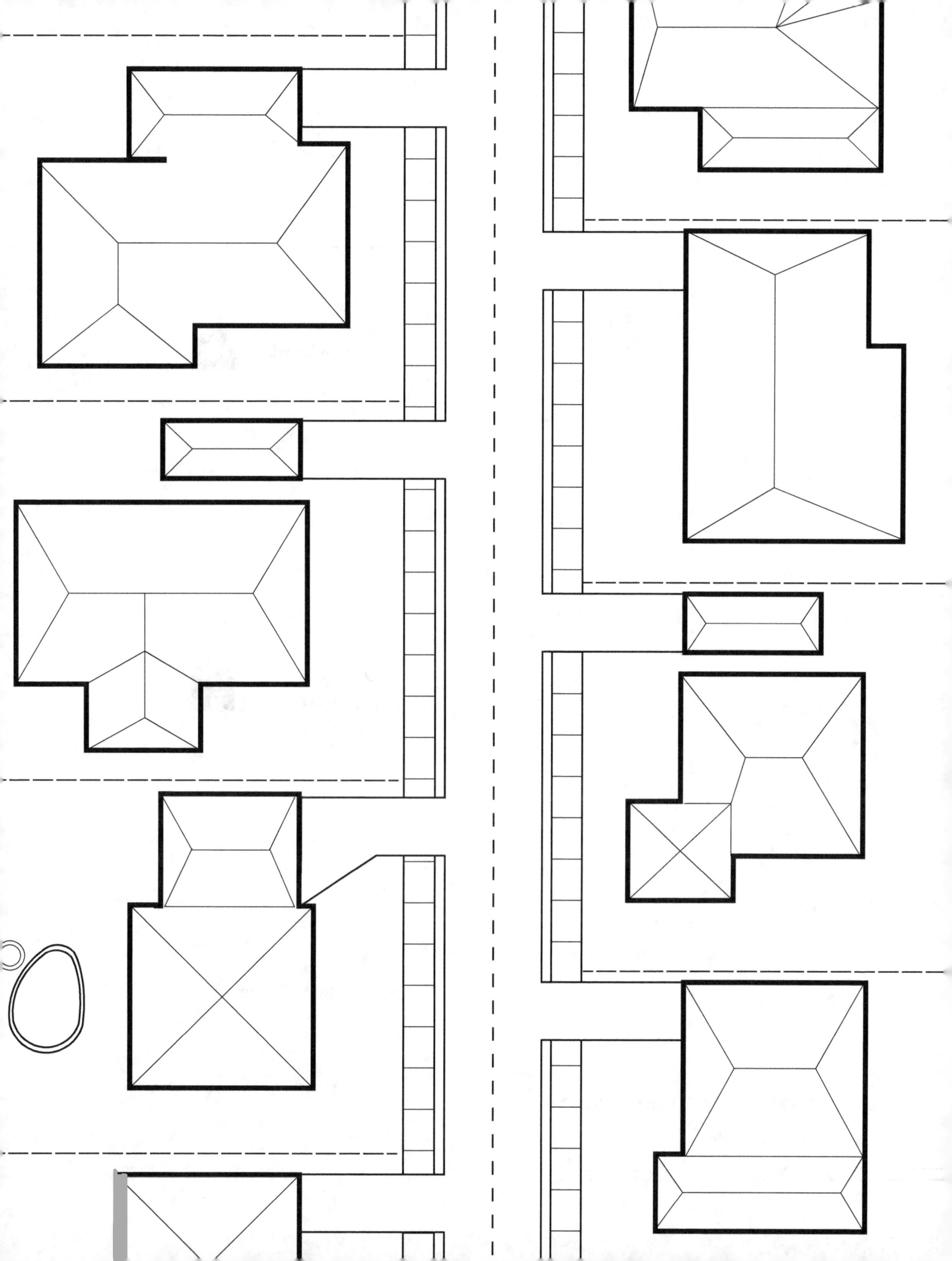

MAP

Story:

_____

Homes & Buildings

_____
_____
_____
_____
_____

Landmarks

_____
_____
_____
_____
_____

Bodies of Water

_____
_____
_____
_____

Provinces/Districts

_____
_____
_____
_____

Lines and Symbols

Scale

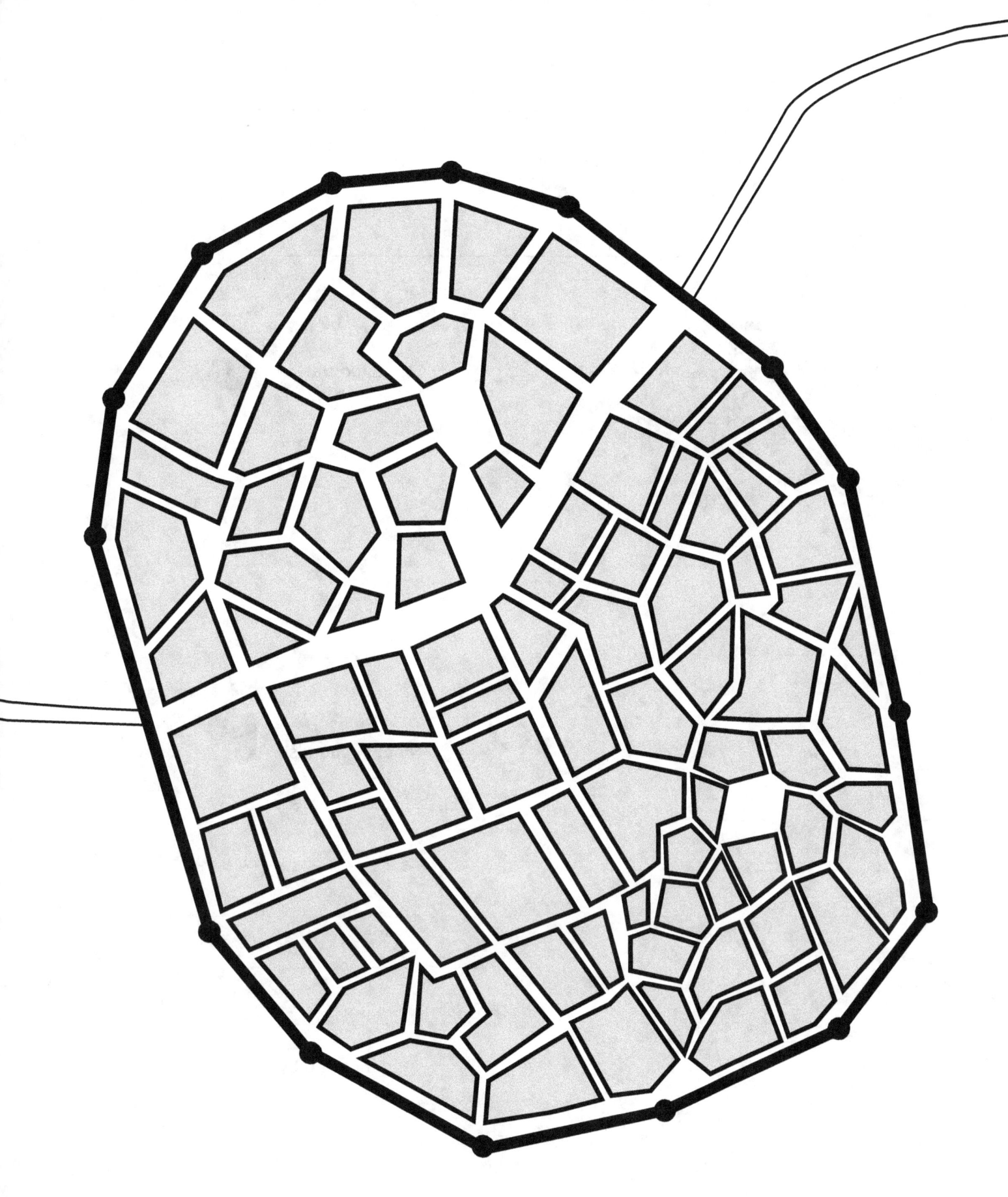

MAP

Story:

_____

Locations

_____
_____
_____
_____
_____
_____
_____
_____
_____

Landmarks

_____
_____
_____
_____

Neighborhoods

_____
_____
_____
_____

Lines and Symbols

Scale

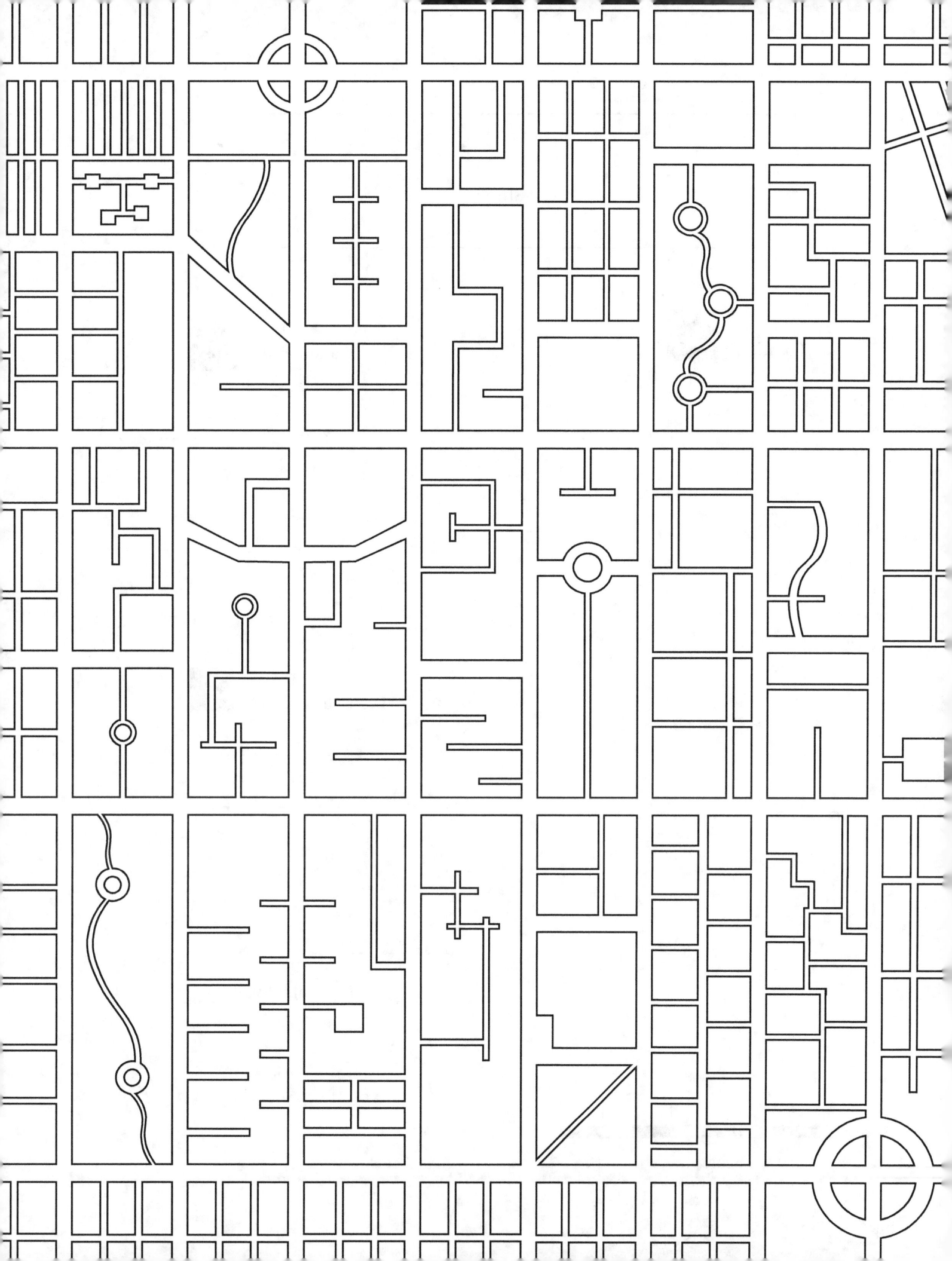

MAP

Story:

_____

Locations

Landmarks

Districts/Zones

Lines and Symbols

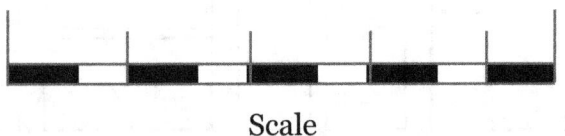

Scale

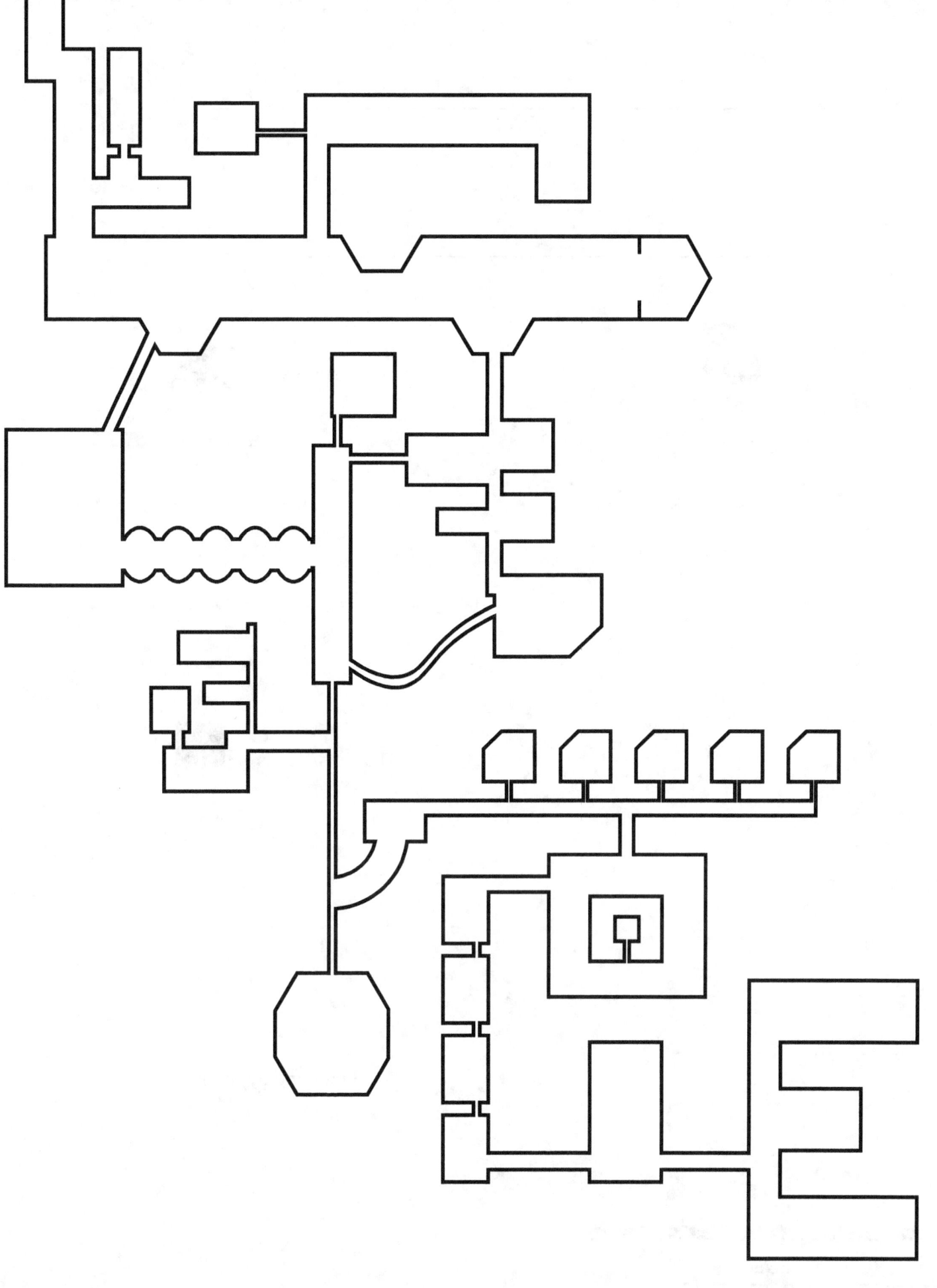

MAP

Story:

_____

Locations

_____
_____
_____
_____
_____
_____
_____
_____

Landmarks

_____
_____
_____
_____

Districts/Zones

_____
_____
_____
_____

Lines and Symbols

Scale

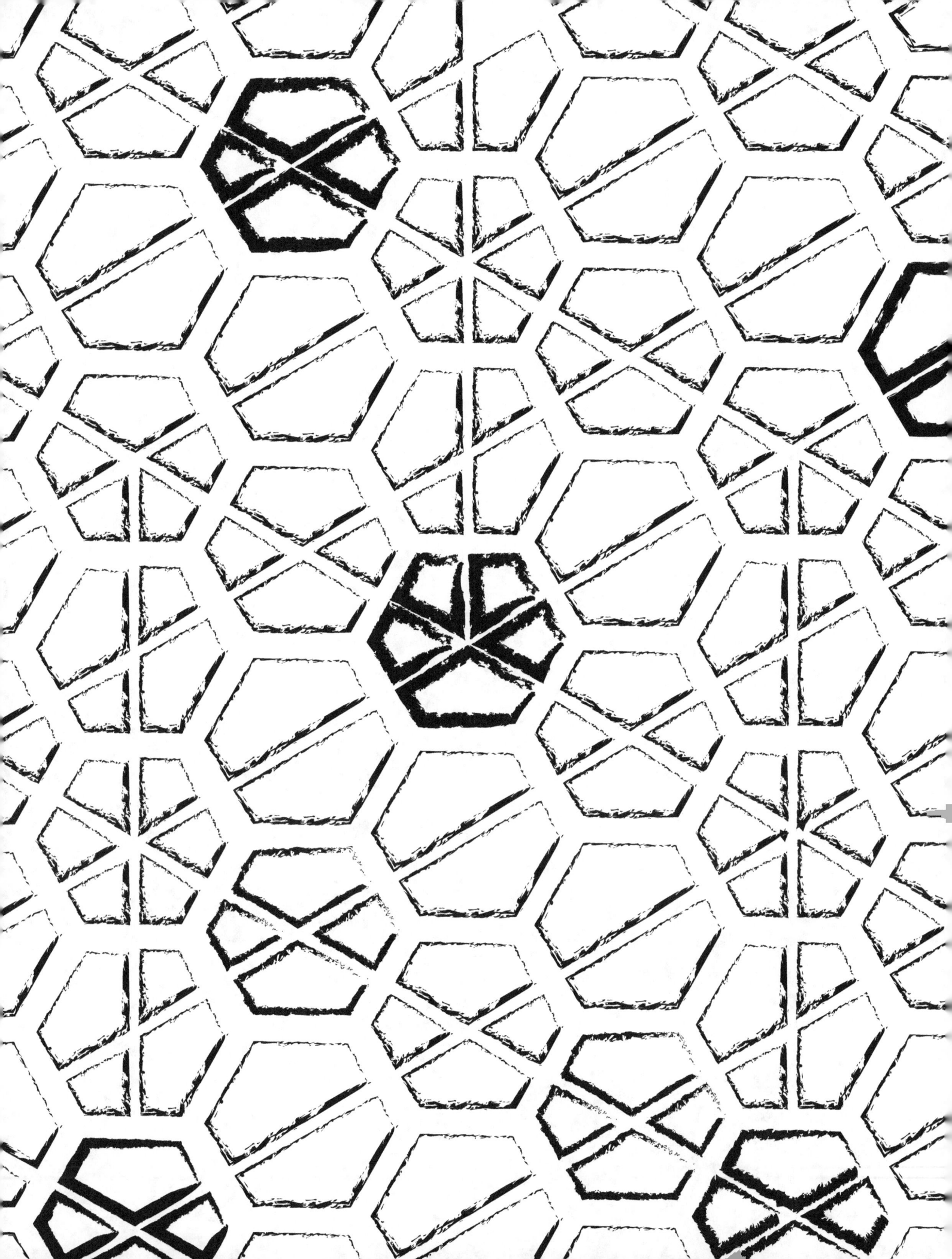

M A P

Story:

Locations

Landmarks

Bodies of Water

Neighborhoods/Districts

Lines and Symbols

Scale

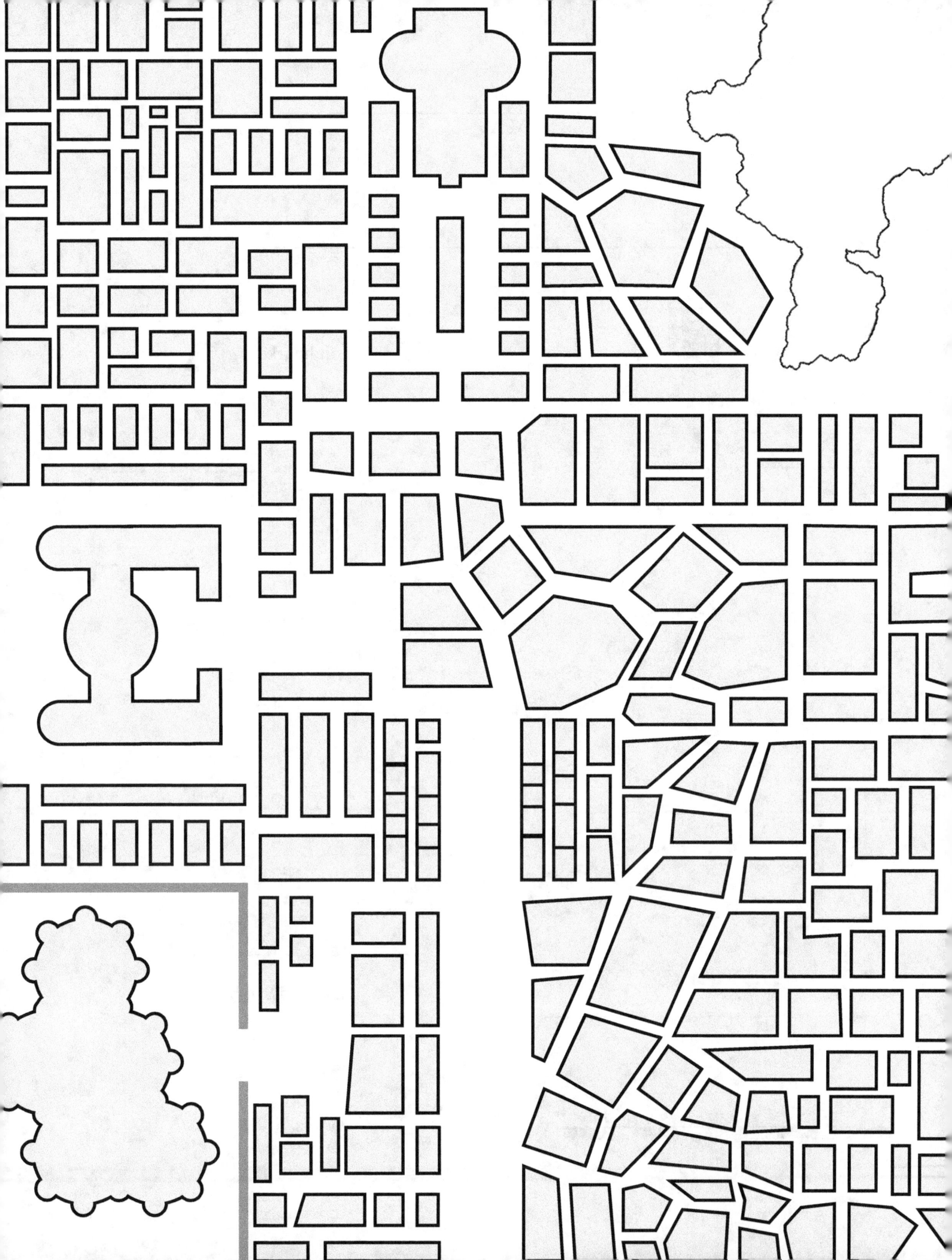

MAP

Story:

Locations

Landmarks

Notes

Lines and Symbols

Scale

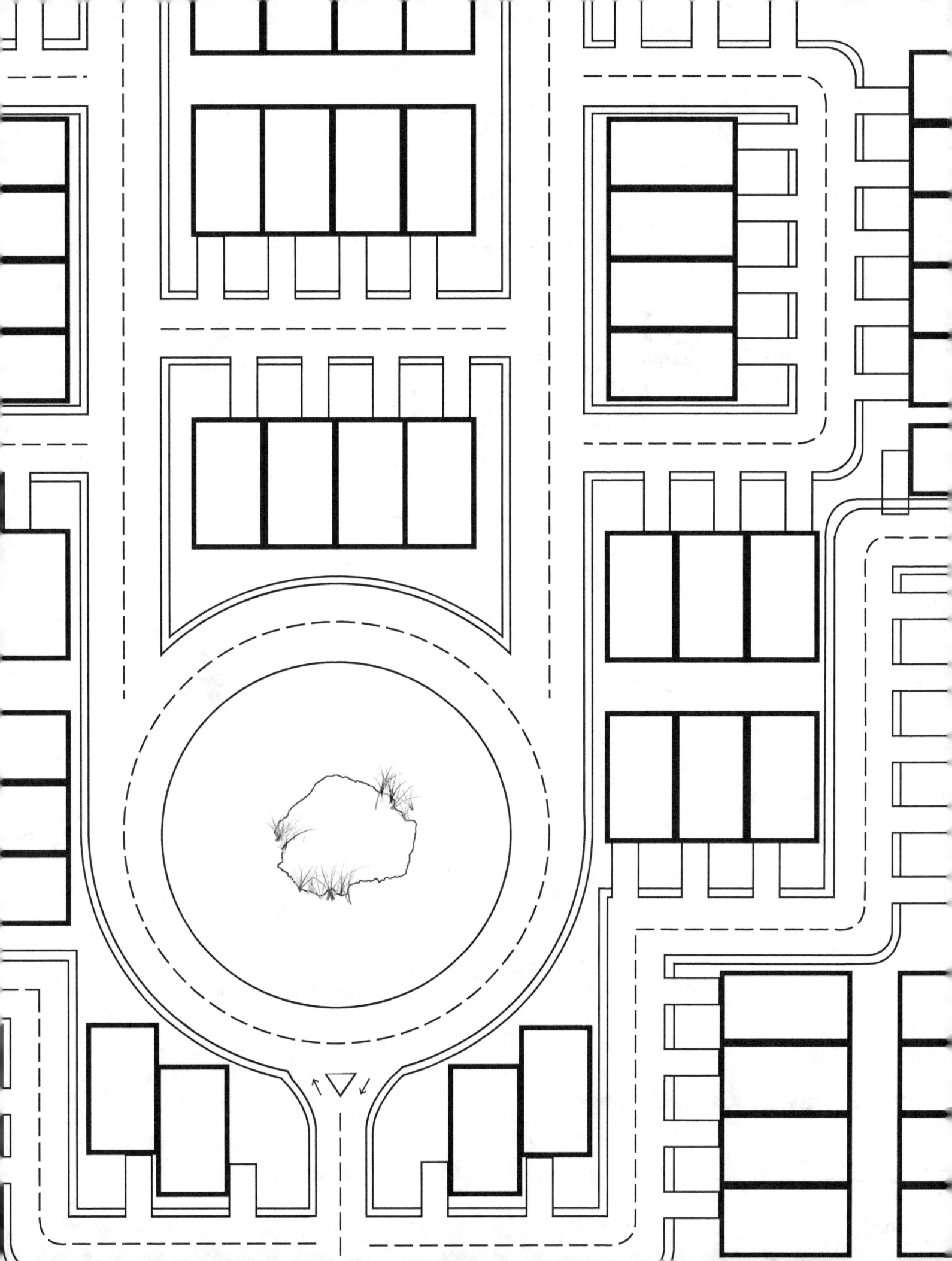

MAP

Story:

_____

Key Locations

_____
_____
_____
_____
_____

Landmarks

_____
_____
_____
_____
_____

Natural Resources

_____
_____
_____
_____
_____

Districts/Zones

_____
_____
_____
_____
_____

Lines and Symbols

Scale

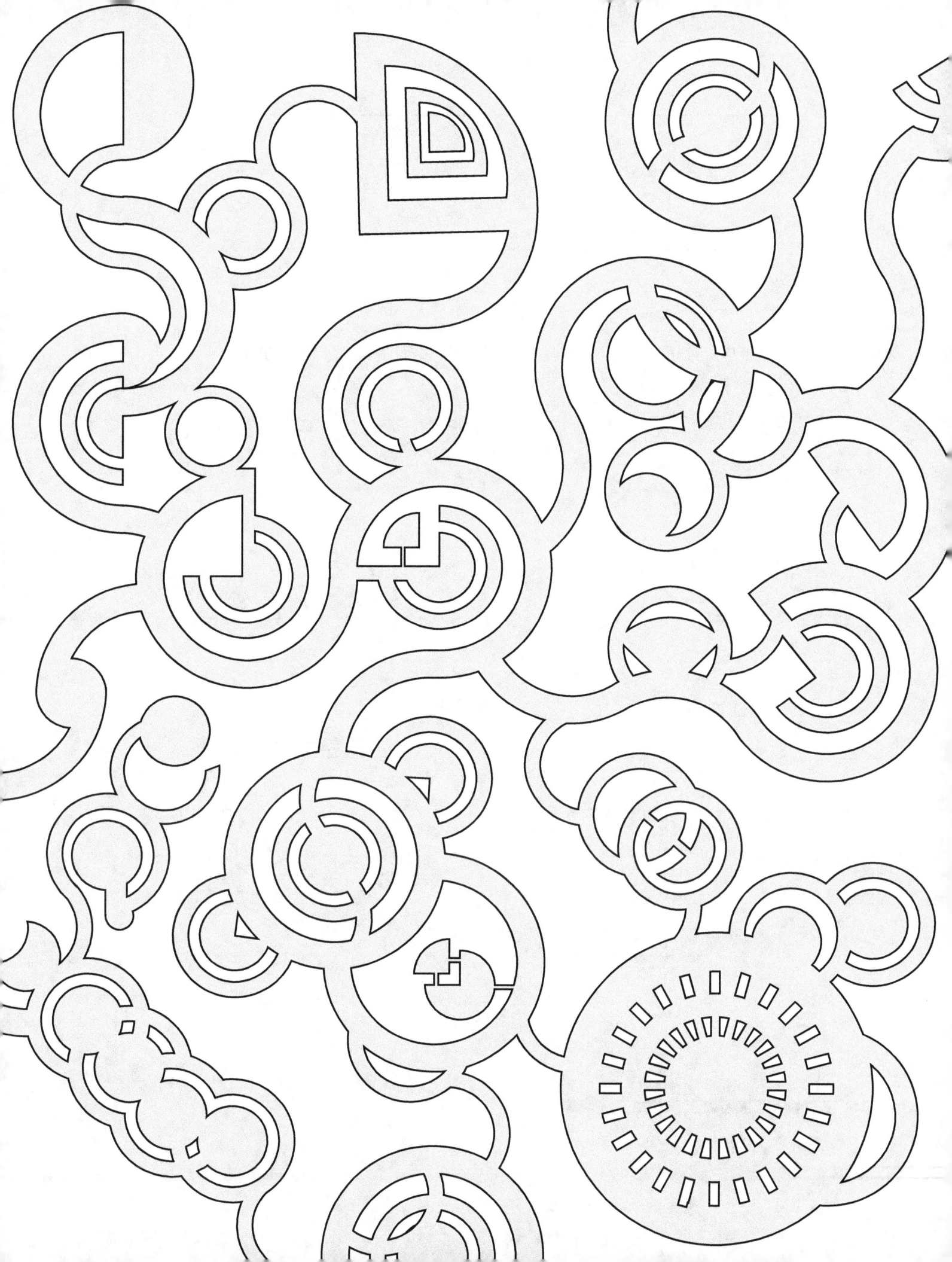

M A P

Story:

_____

Level One

Level Two

Level Three

Level Four

Lines and Symbols

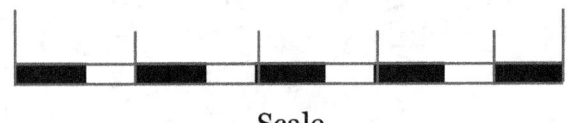

Scale

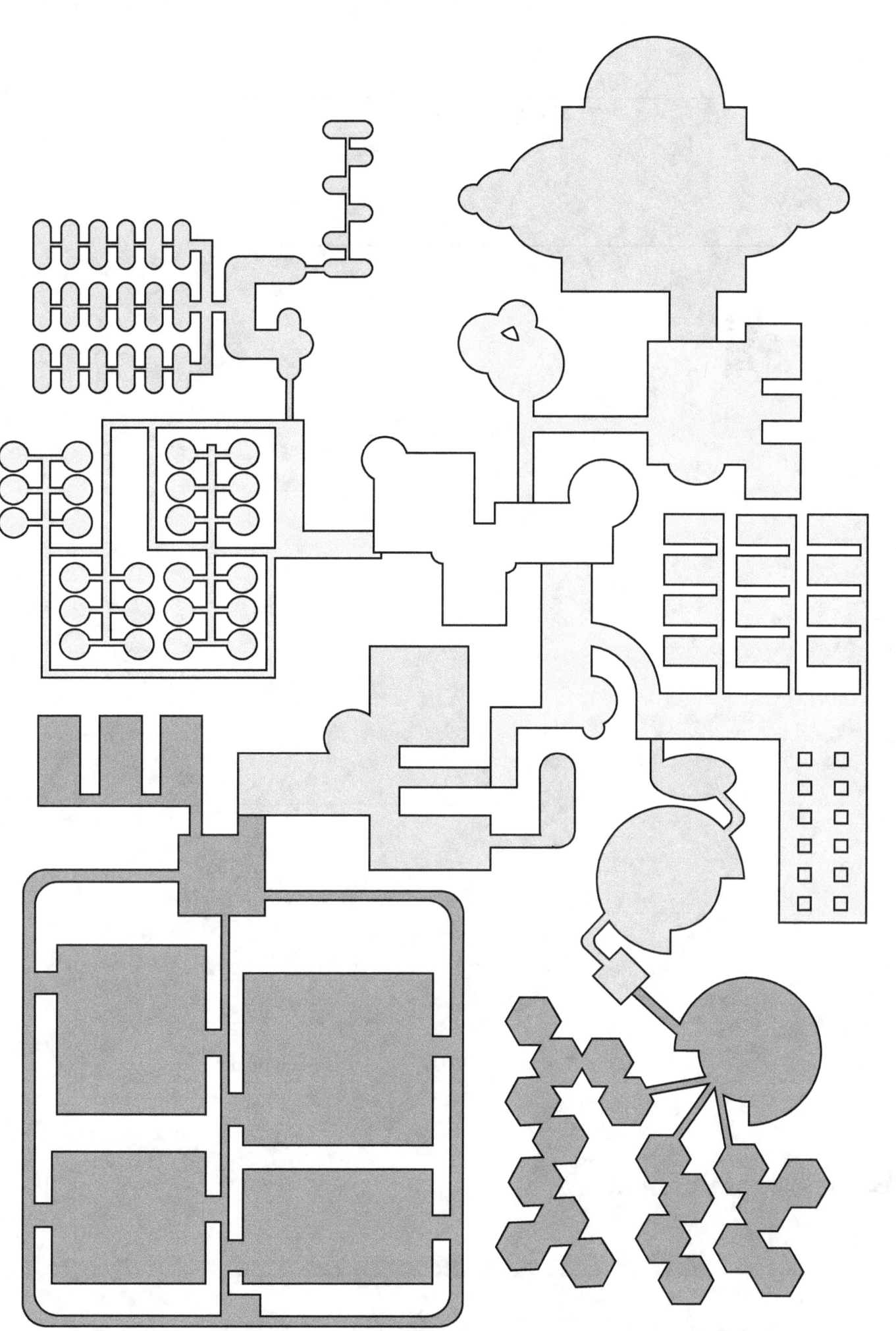

MAP

Story:

Families

Landmarks

Notes

Streets

Lines and Symbols

Scale

108

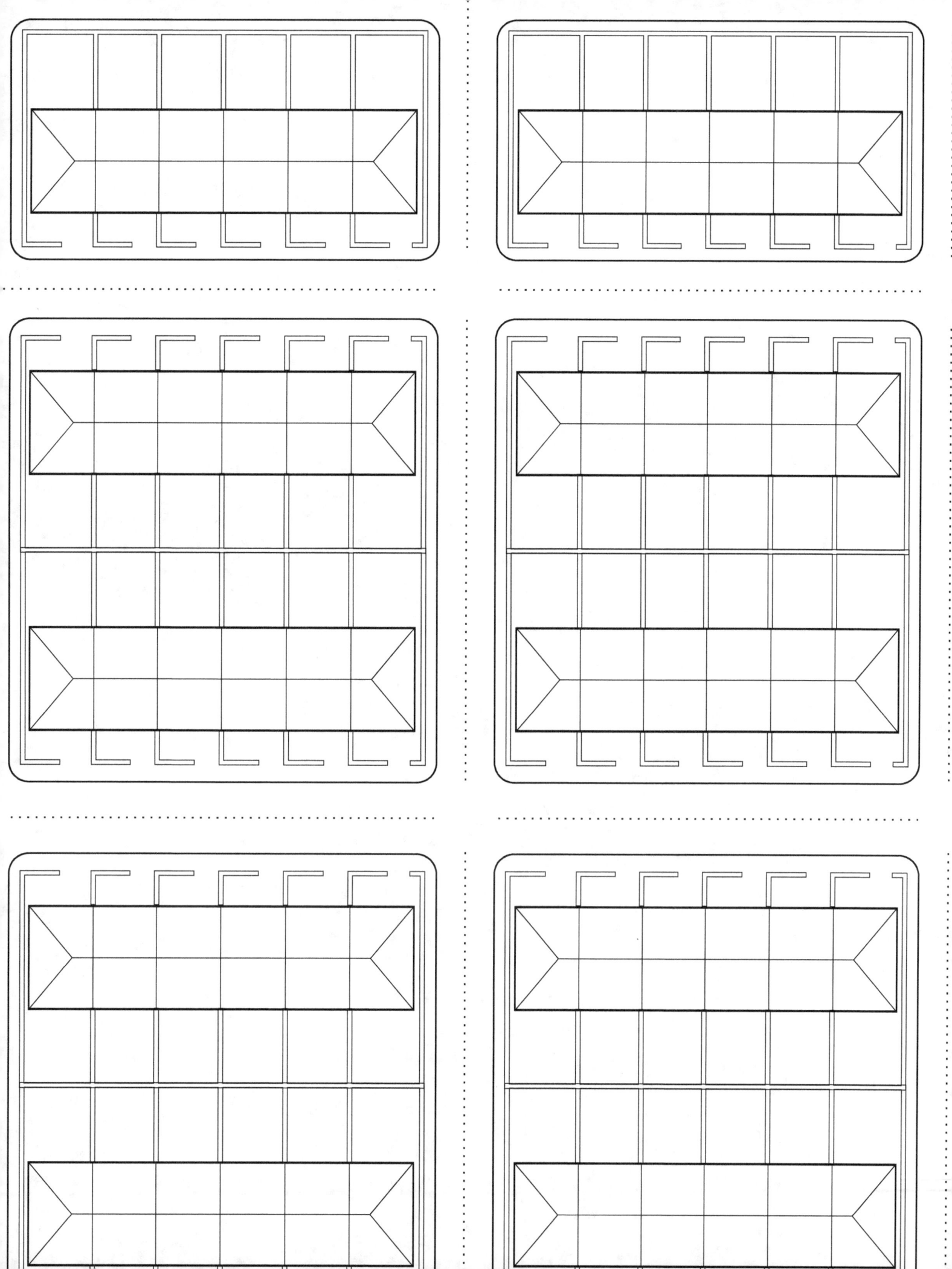

Check out the rest of the series

Maps for Fantasy Creatives

Maps of Fictional Places

Maps to Inspire Storytellers

www.abriamattina.com